A TREASURY OF
QUILTS

BOOKS
FamilyCircle

E D I T O R I A L

Editorial Director *Family Circle Books*	Carol A. Guasti
Associate Editor	Kim E. Gayton
Project Editor	Leslie Gilbert Elman
Book Design	Elizabeth Tunnicliffe
Cover Photo	Bill McGinn
Cover Quilt Designer	Constance Spates
Editorial Production *Coordinator*	Celeste Bantz
Editorial Assistant	Sherieann Holder
Senior Typesetter	Alison Chandler
Typesetting	Maureen Harrington Cheryl Aden

M A R K E T I N G

Director, Family Circle *Books & Licensing*	Margaret Chan-Yip
Direct Marketing Manager	Jill E. Schiffman
Associate Business *Manager*	Carrie Meyerhoff
Administrative Assistant	Laura Berkowitz

Published by The Family Circle, Inc.
110 Fifth Avenue, New York, NY 10011

Copyright® 1991 by The Family Circle, Inc.

Manufactured in the United States of America

10 9 8 7 6 5 4 3 2 1

Library of Congress Cataloging in
Publication Data
Main entry under title:

Family circle a treasury of quilts.
Includes index.
1.Quilts.   2.Crafts.
I.Family Circle, Inc.   II.Title: A Treasury of Quilts

1991   91-70128

ISBN 0-933585-23-3

OTHER BOOKS BY FAMILY CIRCLE

BEST-EVER RECIPES
BEST-EVER RECIPES, VOLUME II

THE BEST OF FAMILY CIRCLE COOKBOOK SERIES
(Pub. Dates: 1985 - 1989)

BUSY COOK'S BOOK

GOOD HEALTH COOKBOOK

MAKE IT COUNTRY
THE COUNTRY KITCHEN
COUNTRY CRAFTS

THE FAMILY CIRCLE CHRISTMAS TREASURY SERIES
(Pub. Dates: 1986 - 1991)

TREASURY OF CHRISTMAS CRAFTS

FAVORITE NEEDLECRAFTS

HINTS, TIPS & SMART ADVICE

To order **FamilyCircle** books, write to Family Circle Books,
110 Fifth Avenue, New York, NY 10011.

To order **FamilyCircle** magazine, write to Family Circle Subscriptions,
110 Fifth Avenue, New York, NY 10011.

TABLE OF CONTENTS

TABLE OF CONTENTS

INTRODUCTION

QUILT-MAKING IS A UNIQUE BLEND OF THE
PRACTICAL AND THE ARTISTIC; A FORM OF
STITCHING BELOVED FOR GENERATIONS. IN
A TREASURY OF QUILTS, YOU'LL FIND BOTH CLASSIC
QUILTS AND NEW TWISTS ON TIME-TESTED IDEAS.
AND, IN KEEPING WITH THE DUAL NATURE OF
QUILTING, A BLEND OF FASCINATING BITS OF
HISTORY AND EASY-TO-FOLLOW DIRECTIONS THAT
WILL MAKE QUILTING A PLEASURE.

SINCE THE DAYS OF ANCIENT EGYPT, PEOPLE HAVE
BEEN STITCHING A PIECE OF BATTING BETWEEN TWO
PIECES OF FABRIC TO MAKE A BEDCOVER. BUT THE
RAISING OF THIS NEEDLEWORK INTO AN ART FORM
IS DUE ALMOST ENTIRELY TO THE INGENUITY AND
CREATIVITY OF THE AMERICAN PIONEER WOMAN.

ALTHOUGH BASIC QUILTING TECHNIQUES WERE
BROUGHT OVER FROM EUROPE, THE SETTLERS OF
THIS COUNTRY HAD TO REINVENT QUILTING AS THEY
STITCHED. THE SCARCITY OF BOTH FABRIC AND
THREAD FORCED QUILTERS TO MAKE MANY
INNOVATIONS IN STITCHING AND PIECEWORK. THE
DESIRE TO CREATE SOMETHING BEAUTIFUL IN AN
OFTEN HARSH ENVIRONMENT INSPIRED THESE
WOMEN TO MAKE QUILTING AN ART.

FAMILY CIRCLE CELEBRATES BOTH THE SPIRIT OF
THESE WOMEN, AND THE UNIQUE BEAUTY OF THEIR
ART. WE HOPE THAT THIS BOOK WILL INSPIRE YOU
TO CARRY ON AN AMERICAN TRADITION WHILE
CREATING NEW HEIRLOOMS FOR YOUR OWN FAMILY.

CLASSIC QUILTS

WHAT MAKES A QUILT A "CLASSIC"?
BY DEFINITION, A CLASSIC IS BORN OF
TRADITION. IT IS THE STANDARD BY
WHICH OTHERS OF ITS KIND ARE
MEASURED. SO IT IS WITH CLASSIC QUILTS.
THESE PATTERNS HAVE BEEN HANDED
DOWN FROM MOTHER TO DAUGHTER
THROUGH GENERATIONS OF
AMERICAN WOMEN. THESE QUILTS
ARE BELOVED BOTH FOR THEIR
BEAUTY AND FOR THE ARTISTRY OF
THEIR CREATORS.

CHAPTER 1

THE CLASSIC QUILTS IN THIS CHAPTER
INCLUDE A WIDE VARIETY OF STYLES,
PATTERNS AND COLORS. YOU'LL FIND
EVERYTHING FROM A COLORFUL
VICTORIAN CRAZY QUILT TO A SIMPLE
AMISH PATTERN. THERE ARE NOTES AND
TIPS TO HELP AND INSPIRE YOU, PLUS
IDEAS FOR EXPANDING AND ADAPTING
THE DESIGNS TO SUIT YOUR OWN TASTE
AND DECOR.

CREATE YOUR OWN CLASSIC QUILT, TO
GIVE TO SOMEONE YOU LOVE, OR TO
TREASURE AS A NEW FAMILY HEIRLOOM
IN YOUR HOME.

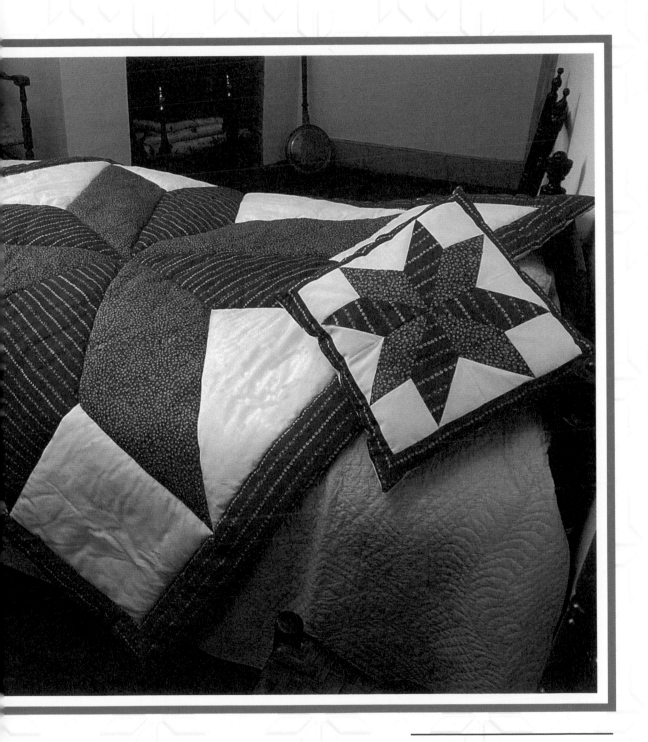

SIMPLE STAR QUILT
(directions, page 4)

SIMPLE STAR QUILT

(Shown on pages 2-3)

EASY:
Achievable by anyone.

DIMENSIONS:
About 58" square

MATERIALS:
- 45-inch-wide fabric:
  1¾ yards of floral
  stripe;
  ¾ yard of calico
- 2¾ yards of 80-inch-
  wide sheeting muslin
  for patches and quilt
  back
- 59-inch square
  of 1-inch-thick
  synthetic batting
- matching sewing
  threads
- crisp cardboard
  or manila folders
- quilting hoop or
  frame (optional)
- Basic Quilting Tools,
  page 137

One of the most basic and popular patterns for quilts is the star. This pattern has more than a hundred variations, and is found both in pieced and appliquéd works. The Simple Star pattern (also known as the Variable Star) consists of a square with eight points radiating outward. The point patches may match or contrast with the center square, all the points may match, or all may be different.

The beauty of this particular quilt is its versatility. The choice of fabric is unlimited. This quilt is lovely made with prints, solids, stripes, checks—your imagination can run wild. Another special feature of this particular Simple Star Quilt is the ease of its construction; this quilt has been designed so that it can be made in approximately 8 hours. If you have always wanted to try your hand at quilting but have been intimidated by the time and difficulty involved, the Simple Star Quilt is the answer. It also is perfect to whip up as a present, or to add a quick touch of beauty to any room in your house. The matching Simple Star Pillow works in tandem with the quilt, or alone as an accent.

Because the Simple Star Quilt is smaller in size than a standard quilt, it is perfect as a cozy throw at the foot of the bed, to spread over the back of a couch for added color, or to hang on the wall as an eye-catching piece of art. It also may be used to cover a small round table.

DIRECTIONS:
(⅜-inch seams allowed)

1. Patterns: Draw two 14-inch squares on the crisp cardboard or manila folders, making sure the squares' corners are 90°, and cut out the squares. Set aside one square. On the second square, draw a diagonal line connecting two opposite points of the square. Draw a second diagonal line ⅜ inch from the first for the seam allowance. Cut along the second line and discard the smaller triangle.

2. Cutting: From the muslin, cut one 66-inch square for the quilt back, four squares and eight triangles. **From the striped fabric,** cut four 4 x 62-inch borders and eight triangles. **From the calico fabric,** cut eight triangles.

3. Quilt Block: With right sides together, seam a striped triangle to a calico triangle along their long edges to make a square. Be sure to place the striped triangle so that the stripes run horizontally. Repeat three times to make a total of four striped/calico squares. Seam the remaining calico and striped triangles to muslin triangles to make 8 more squares.

4. Quilt Top: Following the piecing diagram in Fɪɢ. I, 1, stitch together four quilt blocks to make a row. Repeat to make four rows of quilt blocks. When the four rows of quilt blocks are completed, stitch together the rows to complete the quilt top, following Fɪɢ. I, 1.

5. Border: Fold a border strip in half crosswise and notch the fold to mark the center of the strip. Open the border strip and pin it to one edge of the quilt top, right sides together, matching the border notch to the center seamline of the quilt top. Stitch the border strip to the quilt top. Repeat with a second border strip on the opposite side of the quilt top; do not trim the short ends of the border strips. Repeat with the two remaining border strips on the other edges of the quilt top. Right sides together, fold the quilt top in half on the diagonal, matching the long edges of the borders. Make a mitered corner by pinning together the short ends of two border strips on an angle using the corner of the pieced quilt top as the starting point. Sew the seam, stitching from the inside quilt top point to the outside corner point. Trim the seam allowance to ⅜ inch and press the mitered seam open. Repeat for the three remaining quilt top corners.

6. Assembly: Spread the quilt back, right side up, on a clean, flat surface, and tape down the corners. Center the quilt top, wrong side up, on top of the quilt back. Pin the quilt top to the quilt back in the center. Moving from the center out to the edges of the quilt, smooth out the quilt top and pin the top to the back at the point of each quilt block corner and along the borders. Trim the edges of the quilt top and the quilt back to be even. Stitch the quilt top to the quilt back around three sides and four corners, leaving a 24-inch opening for turning along one side. Remove the pins and turn the quilt right side out.

7. Batting: If the batting needs to be pieced together, spread out the pieces on a clean, flat surface with their edges abutted. Work long cross stitches from one batting piece to the other. Trim the batting flush with the quilt. Slide the batting into the quilt through the opening. Adjust the batting until it lies flat within the quilt; be sure the batting is evenly placed and reaches all the edges and corners of the quilt. Starting at the center of the quilt, pin through all three layers along the quilt block and border seams, placing the pins about 6 inches apart. Turn in the open edges and slipstitch the opening closed (*see Stitch Guide, page 146*).

8. Quilting: By machine, starting at the center of the quilt and using the longest machine stitch, quilt along all the piecing and border seams, removing the pins as you stitch. By hand, place the quilt in a quilting frame or hoop; work from the center outward if you use a hoop. Using a between needle and quilting thread, quilt along all the piecing and border seams; do not remove the pins until the entire quilt top has been quilted.

SIMPLE STAR PILLOW

DIRECTIONS:
(*⅜-inch seams allowed*)

1. Pattern: Draw two 4-inch squares on the crisp cardboard or manila folders, making sure the squares' corners are 90°, and cut out the squares. Set aside one square. On the second square, draw a diagonal line connecting two opposite points of the square. Draw a second diagonal line ⅜ inch from the first for the seam allowance. Cut along the second line and discard the smaller triangle.

2. Cutting: From the muslin, cut one 18-inch-square pillow back, four squares and eight triangles. **From the striped fabric,** cut four 2½ x 18-inch border strips, and eight triangles. **From the calico fabric,** cut eight triangles.

3. Pillow Top: Make the pillow top following the directions in Simple Star Quilt, Steps 3 to 6.

4. Assembly: Stitch the pillow top to the pillow back around three sides and four corners, leaving a 6-inch opening for turning. Turn the pillow cover right side out, and stuff the pillow firmly. Turn in the open edges and slipstitch the opening closed (*see Stitch Guide, page 146*).

EASY:
Achievable by anyone.

DIMENSIONS:
About 17" square

MATERIALS:
- 45-inch-wide fabric: ¼ yard of striped calico for patches and border; ⅛ yard of print calico for patches
- ½ yard of 30-inch-wide muslin for the patches and quilt back
- synthetic stuffing
- matching sewing threads
- crisp cardboard or manila folders
- Basic Quilting Tools, page 137

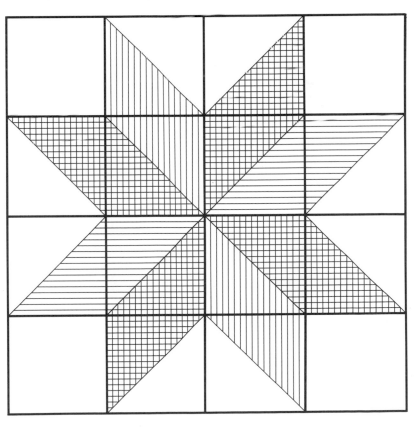

FIG. I, 1
QUILT AND PILLOW
PIECING DIAGRAM

EVENING STAR QUILT

AVERAGE:
For those with some experience in quilting.

DIMENSIONS:
About 97 x 109½"

MATERIALS:
- 45-inch-wide solid color cotton fabric: 5 yards of orange; 3¼ yards of green; 1½ yards each of light blue and dark blue; 8¼ yards of gold for quilt back
- matching quilting threads
- synthetic batting, pieced as needed to measure 100 x 112 inches
- crisp cardboard or manila folders
- water-soluble fabric marking pen
- quilting hoop or frame
- Basic Quilting Tools, page 137

Evening Star, sometimes called Economy Star, is a variation on the Simple Star quilt pattern, and is one of the easiest pieced star patterns. This lovely quilt has been embellished by the use of three solid colors for the pieced star blocks. Many antique Evening Star quilts were made with just two colors—one for the points and one for the center and surrounding pieces.

The Evening Star Quilt shown in the photo at right, actually is a reproduction of a gorgeous quilt made in 1834 which is on display at the Winterthur Museum and Gardens in Delaware. The original quilt is hanging on the quilt rack next to the bed in the photo. Our quilt is backed with a radiant golden fabric just like the original quilt. We have extended the orange border from the original dimensions so the quilt would fit on modern larger-size beds.

Although the Evening Star has a simple piecing pattern, the quilting designs are more intricate than the seam quilting done on the Simple Star Quilt (directions, page 4). The quilting designs on a simple patchwork quilt add subtle visual interest to the finished project. Because the piecework is relatively easy, this quilt pattern lends itself to some wonderful variations in color and fabric.

DIRECTIONS:

(¼-inch seams allowed, except where noted)
Note 1: *The quilt top is assembled from squares, right triangles, and borders. The patchwork is machine-stitched; the quilting is done by hand.*
Note 2: *To use fabric economically, cut the borders first. Cut the patches with their edges abutting, and cut pairs of matching triangles by cutting a square in half on the diagonal.*

1. Patterns: Using the dimensions given in Fig. I, 2A *(page 8)*, draw separate patterns for each of the four triangles on the crisp cardboard or manila folders. Label and cut out the triangle patterns. Draw a 10½-inch, 5½-inch and a 3-inch square, making sure their corners are 90°, and cut out the square patterns. Trace the full-size petal quilting pattern in Fig. I, 2B *(page 8)* onto the crisp cardboard or manila folders, and cut out.

2. Cutting: From the orange fabric, cut two 17½ x 85-inch side borders, one 4½ x 91-inch top border, one 17½ x 91-inch bottom border and 192 A triangles. **From the green fabric,** cut two 2¼ x 108-inch borders, one 2¼ x 97-inch border, fifteen 10½-inch squares, sixteen D triangles and four C triangles. **From the dark blue fabric,** cut six 2 x 54-inch strips and seam together to make two 2 x 106½-inch side borders and one 2 x 94-inch bottom border, then cut 96 B triangles. **From the light blue fabric,** cut twenty-four 5½-inch squares and ninety-six 3-inch squares. **From the gold fabric,** cut two 45 x 115-inch panels and two 18 x 58-inch panels for quilt back.

3. Quilt Block: *(Press all seams toward the darker color patch.)* Sew the long edges of two orange A triangles to the short edges of a dark blue B triangle; the raw edges of the patches will not match, but the seamlines will. Repeat until you have 96 orange/blue rectangles. Sew the long edge of an orange/blue rectangle to one side of a 5½-inch light blue square, placing the rectangle with the orange points radiating out from the light blue square *(see photo)*. Repeat on the remaining three sides of the light blue square. Sew the 3-inch light blue squares to the short ends of the orange/blue rectangles to make a complete quilt block. Repeat to make 23 more quilt blocks.

(Continued on page 8)

EVENING STAR QUILT

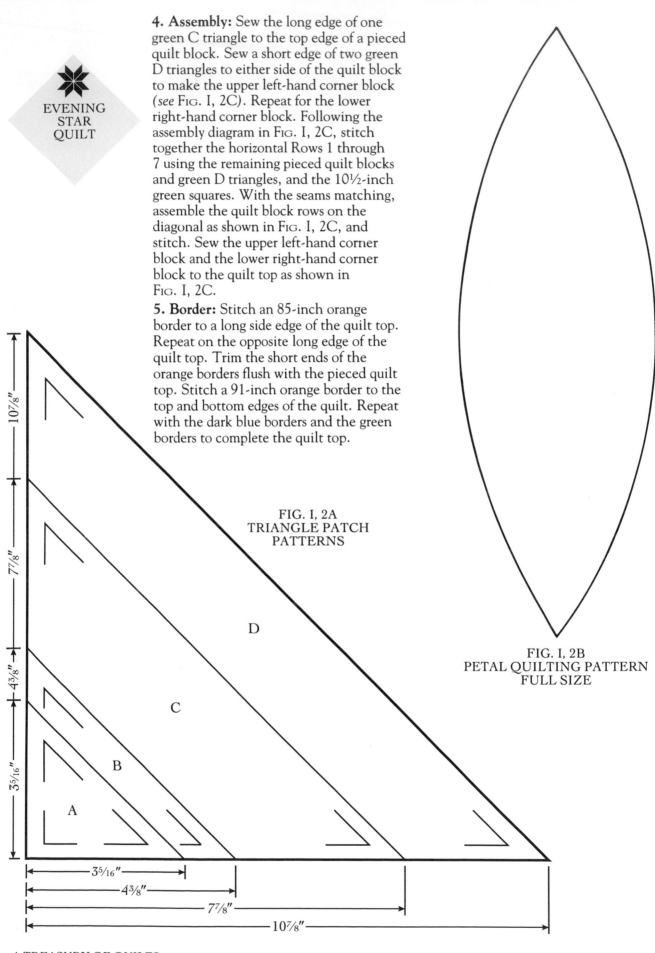

4. Assembly: Sew the long edge of one green C triangle to the top edge of a pieced quilt block. Sew a short edge of two green D triangles to either side of the quilt block to make the upper left-hand corner block (*see* Fig. I, 2C). Repeat for the lower right-hand corner block. Following the assembly diagram in Fig. I, 2C, stitch together the horizontal Rows 1 through 7 using the remaining pieced quilt blocks and green D triangles, and the 10½-inch green squares. With the seams matching, assemble the quilt block rows on the diagonal as shown in Fig. I, 2C, and stitch. Sew the upper left-hand corner block and the lower right-hand corner block to the quilt top as shown in Fig. I, 2C.

5. Border: Stitch an 85-inch orange border to a long side edge of the quilt top. Repeat on the opposite long edge of the quilt top. Trim the short ends of the orange borders flush with the pieced quilt top. Stitch a 91-inch orange border to the top and bottom edges of the quilt. Repeat with the dark blue borders and the green borders to complete the quilt top.

EVENING
STAR
QUILT

FIG. I, 2A
TRIANGLE PATCH
PATTERNS

10⅞"

7⅞"

4⅜"

3⁵⁄₁₆"

D

C

B

A

3⁵⁄₁₆"

4⅜"

7⅞"

10⅞"

FIG. I, 2B
PETAL QUILTING PATTERN
FULL SIZE

6. Marking: Draw intersecting diagonal lines connecting the corners of the 5½-inch square pattern. Place the petal pattern on top of one of the diagonal lines with a petal point at the center "X" on the square. Trace the petal onto the cardboard square. Repeat three times to complete the pattern. Cut out the petal shapes to make a stencil-like pattern. Spread the quilt top, right side up, on a clean, flat surface, and tape down the corners. Place the petal pattern on top of a light blue center square, and trace the petal design onto the fabric using the fabric marking pen. Repeat until all the blue center squares are marked. Mark the solid green patches and the orange borders with 1-inch squares placed parallel to the edges of the pieced quilt blocks. Remove the tape.

7. Quilt Back: Trim the selvages from the gold fabric pieces. Using a ½-inch seam allowance, stitch together the 18 x 58-inch pieces along a short end to make an 18 x 115-inch rectangle. Stitch together the 45 x 115-inch pieces along a long edge. Stitch the 18 x 115-inch rectangle to the combined rectangle along a long edge to complete the quilt back. The quilt back should measure approximately 106 x 115 inches. Press all the seams to one side.

8. Basting: If the batting needs to be pieced together, spread the pieces on a clean, flat surface with their edges abutted. Work long cross stitches from one batting piece to the other. Spread the quilt back, wrong side up, on the clean, flat surface, and tape down the corners. Place the batting on top of the quilt back. Starting in the center and working out toward the edges, smooth the batting over the quilt back. Place the quilt top, centered and right side up, on top of the batting. Starting at the center, working straight out to each edge and diagonally out to each corner, baste through all three layers using long stitches. Add more rows of basting about 6 inches apart, working both vertical and horizontal rows.

9. Quilting: Place the quilt in a quilting hoop or frame. Start quilting from the center and work outward. Use quilting thread that matches each fabric used in the quilt. Quilt, using small running stitches through all three layers, in the following order: four-petal pattern centered in each large light blue square, ⅛ inch inside the seamlines of the orange triangles;

FIG. I, 2C QUILT ASSEMBLY DIAGRAM

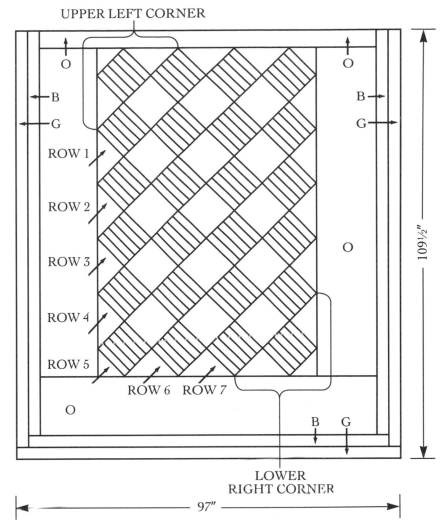

UPPER LEFT CORNER

ROW 1
ROW 2
ROW 3
ROW 4
ROW 5
ROW 6   ROW 7

109½"

97"

LOWER RIGHT CORNER

= QUILT BLOCKS

O = ORANGE
G = GREEN
B = BLUE

the 1-inch diagonal square pattern on the large green squares and the orange, green and blue borders, ⅛ inch inside both seams of the orange borders.

10. Binding: Trim the batting flush with the quilt top. Trim the quilt back to extend 1 inch beyond the quilt top on all sides. Fold under the raw edges of the quilt back ½ inch, then fold it again over the quilt top to be the binding, and pin the binding in place. Slipstitch the binding to the quilt top, mitering the corners (*see Stitch Guide, page 146*). Remove the basting to finish.

ROMAN SQUARE QUILT

AVERAGE:
For those with some experience in quilting.

DIMENSIONS:
About 90 x 110″

MATERIALS:
- 45-inch-wide fabric: 1 yard each of six different print fabrics; 1 yard of solid tan; 9½ yards of blue print for patches, outer border and quilt back
- matching sewing threads
- synthetic batting, pieced as needed to measure 91 x 111 inches
- six-strand embroidery floss
- Basic Quilting Tools, page 137

Roman Square is a pattern that can be pieced with fairly small scraps of fabric. Early quilters used the Roman Square's fabric requirements and pattern flexibility to their advantage.

Most antique samples of Roman Square quilts are made from dozens of different fabrics assembled in 4-patch blocks. But there also are antique Roman Square quilts in which three fabric strips are joined to make a block. The three-strip blocks are then joined together with solid color strips in between and around them to create a windowpane effect.

We chose to use only seven fabrics, cut in narrow strips and assembled in 7-patch blocks. Traditionally, it was common to arrange the fabric strips within a square from light to dark to create an overall optical effect. We created 63 identical blocks for our quilt and, by alternating the vertical and horizontal placement of the quilt blocks, we created a repeating stairway effect. Notice how the dark orange and blue border print strips zigzag across the quilt.

As with most quilting patterns, there are endless variations you can create from the basic Roman Square pattern. Remember, every quilter does things just a little bit differently from her neighbor; the personal vision of a quilter is part of the beauty of quilting.

DIRECTIONS:
(¼-inch seams allowed, except where noted)

1. Cutting: From the tan fabric, cut nine 3½ x 45-inch strips for the inner border. **From the blue print fabric,** cut two 45 x 93-inch pieces and one 28 x 93-inch piece for the quilt back, and nine 6 x 45-inch strips for the outer border. **From each of the six print fabrics and the remaining blue print fabric,** cut sixteen 2 x 45-inch strips.

2. Quilt Block: Place seven of the 2-inch-wide strips, one from each fabric, side by side to create broad stripes of blending colors. For the quilt in the photo on page 11, we placed the strips in the following order: three blue strips, an off-white print strip, and three orange/gold strips. Stitch together the strips along their long edges (*see* Fig. I, 3A, *page 12*) to make a rectangle measuring 11 x 45 inches. Repeat to make a total of 16 rectangles, keeping the strips in the same color order. Starting from one short end of a rectangle, mark off four blocks measuring 11 inches, and cut the blocks apart. Repeat with the remaining rectangles. You should have 64 blocks. Set aside one quilt block for another purpose.

3. Assembly: Place seven quilt blocks side by side, starting with a quilt block with the strips set vertically, and placing alternating blocks horizontally (*see* Fig. I, 3B, *Row 1, page 12*). Stitch together the quilt blocks. Press all the seams to one side. Repeat to make four more rows of quilt blocks following the Row 1 placement pattern. Place seven more quilt blocks side by side, starting with a quilt block with the strips set horizontally, and placing alternating blocks vertically (*see* Fig. I, 3B, *Row 2*). Stitch together the quilt blocks. Repeat to make three more rows of quilt blocks following the Row 2 placement pattern. Stitch together the quilt block rows, working from the top edge of the quilt to the bottom edge, and alternating Rows 1 and 2.

4. Borders: Stitch together the short ends of the nine tan fabric strips to make a single inner border strip. Stitch the inner border strip to one long edge of the patchwork, matching one short end of the border to the bottom edge of the patchwork, and trimming the opposite

(Continued on page 12)

ROMAN SQUARE QUILT

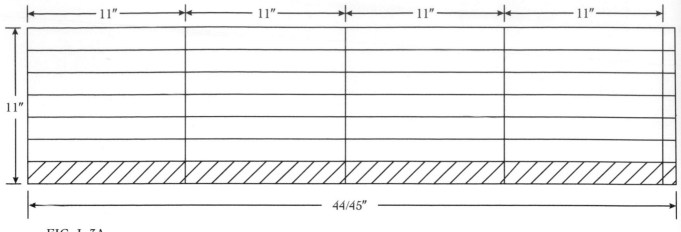

FIG. I, 3A
STRIP ASSEMBLY

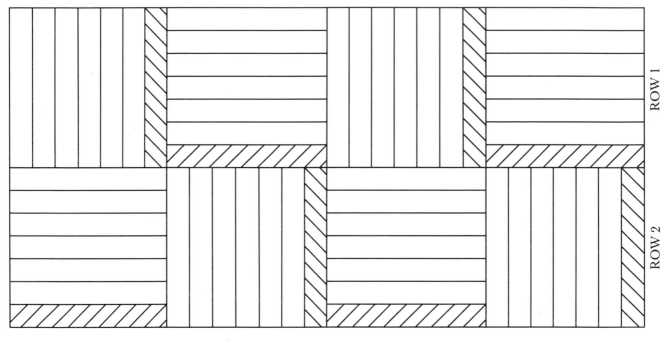

FIG. I, 3B
QUILT BLOCK
PLACEMENT

ROW 1

ROW 2

⬚ = ORANGE

short end of the border flush with the top edge of the quilt. Repeat on the opposite long edge. Press the seams toward the center of the patchwork. Repeat with the remaining inner border strip at the top and bottom edges, trimming the ends flush with the side borders. Stitch together the short ends of the nine blue border strips to make a single outer border strip. Stitch the outer border to the quilt in the same way as the inner border, and press the seams toward the outside edge of the quilt top.

5. Basting: If the batting needs to be pieced together, spread the pieces on a clean, flat surface with their edges abutted. Work long cross stitches from one batting piece to the other. Spread the quilt top, wrong side up, on a clean, flat surface, and tape down the corners. Place the batting, centered, on the quilt top, and trim the edges of the batting flush with the edges of the quilt top. Starting at the center, working straight out to each edge and diagonally out to each corner, baste through both layers using long stitches. Add more rows of basting about 6 inches apart, working both vertical and horizontal rows. Remove the tape.

6. Binding: Stitch together the three blue quilt back pieces along their long edges, placing the narrow piece in the center. Press the seams to one side. Spread the quilt back, right side up, on a clean, flat surface, and tape down the corners. Place the basted quilt top and batting, batting side up and centered, on top of the quilt back. Pin-baste all three layers together from the center straight out to each edge, and diagonally out to each corner. Add more rows of pins about 6 inches apart. Trim the quilt back flush with the quilt top/batting layer. Remove the tape. Using a ½-inch seam allowance, stitch together all three layers around three sides and four corners, leaving an 18-inch opening on one side for turning. Remove the basting pins and basting thread, and turn the quilt right side out. Turn in the open edges and slipstitch the opening closed (*see Stitch Guide, page 146*).

7. Tie Quilting: Spread the quilt, right side up, on a clean, flat surface. Pin-baste again through all three layers, placing a pin at each corner of a quilt block. Use a curved needle or a darner needle; a curved needle will make the stitching easier. Thread the needle with a length of the embroidery floss; do not knot the floss. Starting at the center of the quilt, and working from the top, take a short stitch through all three layers at the corner of a quilt block; leave a 2-inch tail of floss. Take another stitch on top of the first. Cut the floss about 2 inches above the stitches. Tie the floss tails into a square knot (*see How To Tie A Square Knot, page 145*), and trim the ends to ½ inch. Repeat across the quilt, making ties at each corner of all the quilt blocks. Remove the basting pins.

A PIECE OF QUILTING HISTORY

Over 500 years ago, people discovered that a sheet of cotton or wool batting sandwiched between two pieces of fabric provided more warmth and protection than the fabric alone. To hold the batting in place between the pieces of fabric, they used rows of tiny stitches—and the art of quilting was born.

Warriors in the Far East, Europe and North Africa found that quilted vests and jackets helped shield them from the flying spears and arrows of their enemies. Even horses were decked out for battle in quilted blankets. In the icy mountain regions of ancient China, people wore quilted clothing for warmth. In the dark, dank castles of Europe the nobles slept under quilted bedcovers.

The earliest quilted bedcovers were simply sheets of plain fabric decorated with quilting alone—no patchwork or appliqués. The quilting motifs varied from relatively simple repeating patterns to very elaborate stitchery. The entire bedcover would be worked with tiny stitches placed very close together.

In Europe, where textiles were easy to come by, quilted bedcovers often were made from rich fabrics. In 1540, Catherine Howard, the fifth wife of Henry VIII, included 23 silk quilts in her wedding trousseau. In the 1600's, European fashion featured bedcovers made from opulent fabrics and lace, and quilting had become a highly developed craft.

Despite their disdain for worldly possessions, the Puritans who came to the New World brought a European sense of beauty with them. Since fabric was in short supply, they created bedcovers by piecing together fabric scraps, then decorated them with beautiful—and practical!—quilting.

ROMAN SQUARE QUILT

BOW TIE QUILT

BOW TIE QUILT

This classic quilt design is a favorite of the Amish, who make bow tie quilts in their signature bold solid colors. The piecing for the Bow Tie Quilt is a bit tricky; this project is not recommended for beginning quilters.

We chose a cheery red, white and blue color scheme for our bedcover. The quilt fits a modern double bed with enough extra cover at the top to tuck under the pillows. The quilting design is merely a grid pattern and an outline of the bow tie patches, in keeping with the simplicity of the patchwork design.

The bow tie pattern is extremely versatile. Simply rotating the patchwork squares can create a completely different look. All the bow ties in our quilt are facing the same direction, which creates a diagonal line. If you prefer, you can alternate the bow ties to make V shapes, or diamond shapes from a square of four bow ties.

The bow tie pattern lends itself to dozens of color and fabric combinations. If you have a surplus of fabric scraps, make every bow tie from a different fabric and use a plain muslin or solid color cotton fabric for the background. For a luxuriously opulent quilt, use old silk neckties to make the bow tie patches and velvet for the background fabric.

DIRECTIONS:
(¼-inch seams allowed)

Note: *Before cutting out the pattern pieces, straighten the cut ends of all the fabrics and trim away the selvages.*

1. Pattern: Trace the full-size patch pattern in FIG. I, 4A *(page 17)* onto the crisp cardboard or manila folder. Cut out the patch pattern.

2. Cutting: From the blue fabric, cut out two hundred fifty-two 3½-inch squares. Place the patch pattern on top of a marked square with the straight edges matching, and trace the cut-off corner onto the fabric. Repeat for the remaining marked squares. Cut out 252 patches. **From the white fabric,** cut out 252 patches in the same way as the blue patches. Also, cut two 21 x 88-inch side borders, two 45 x 117-inch quilt back pieces, one 14 x 117-inch quilt back piece, one 21 x 99-inch bottom border and one 5 x 99-inch top border. **From the red fabric,** cut off four 2-inch-wide border strips the length of the fabric, one hundred twenty-six 2-inch squares, and enough 2½-inch-wide bias strips to make about 12 yards of bias binding, pieced as needed.

3. Quilt Block: With right sides together, pin the angled short edge of a white patch centered over one edge of a red patch (the ends won't match). Stitch together the patches, starting and stopping at the seamline, so the seam allowances are left open *(see FIG. I, 4B, page 17)*. Center and stitch a second white patch to the opposite red edge. Repeat with two blue patches on the remaining two red edges. With the edges even, and starting from the corner point of the red patch, stitch the white and blue patches together along their abutting seams *(see FIG. I, 4C, page 17)* to complete the quilt block. Press all the seams toward the darker fabric. Repeat to make 125 more quilt blocks. With edges even and seams matching, stitch together the quilt blocks in fourteen horizontal rows of nine blocks each. Starting at the top edge of the quilt, with edges even and seams matching, stitch together the fourteen horizontal rows of quilt blocks to make the quilt top.

AVERAGE:
For those with some experience in quilting.

DIMENSIONS:
About 98 x 112"

MATERIALS:
- 45-inch-wide fabric: 15 yards of white broadcloth or unbleached muslin; 2⅜ yards of blue print; 2½ yards of red print
- matching sewing threads
- matching quilting threads
- two pieces of 90 x 108-inch synthetic batting
- white dressmaker's pencil
- No. 8 or No. 10 quilting needle
- crisp cardboard or manila folder
- quilting frame or hoop
- Basic Quilting Tools, page 137

4. Border: Stitch a red border strip to a long edge of the patchwork assembly, and trim the border ends flush with the patchwork edge. Repeat on the opposite side of the patchwork assembly. Stitch a red border to the top and bottom edges of the patchwork assembly, and trim the top and bottom border edges flush with the red side borders. Stitch the 88-inch white side borders to the red side borders, and trim the ends of the white borders flush with the red top and bottom borders. Stitch the white top and bottom borders to the red top and bottom borders. Trim the white top border flush with the white side borders. Trim the white bottom border flush with the red side borders.

5. Marking: Using the white dressmaker's pencil, sharpened, lightly mark the red and white borders with diagonal lines spaced 1½ inches apart. Repeat, making the second set of lines perpendicular to the first set of lines to form 1½-inch squares.

6. Quilt Back: Stitch together the white quilt back pieces along their long edges, placing the narrow piece between the two wider pieces. The quilt back should measure approximately 103 x 117 inches.

7. Basting: To piece together the batting, spread the pieces on a clean, flat surface with their long edges abutted. Work long cross stitches from one batting piece to the other. The combined batting piece should measure approximately 108 x 118 inches. Spread the quilt back, wrong side up, on a clean, flat surface, and tape down the corners. Place the batting on top of the quilt back; the batting will extend beyond the edges of the quilt back. Place the quilt top, centered and right side up, on top of the batting. Starting at the center, working straight out to each edge and diagonally out to each corner, baste through all three layers using long stitches. Add more rows of basting about 8 inches apart, working both vertical and horizontal rows. Remove the tape.

8. Quilting: Place the quilt in a quilting hoop or frame. Start quilting from the center and work outward. Use the quilting thread that matches each fabric used in the quilt. Using small running stitches through all three layers, quilt about ¼ inch inside the edges of the blue and white patches. Continue until all the blue and white patches have been quilted. Then quilt on the marked squares in the white and red borders.

9. Binding: Trim the quilt back and batting flush with the quilt top. Fold the red bias strip in half, wrong sides facing, and press. Keeping the bias strip folded, pin the bias strip to the quilt, right sides together and raw edges even. Stitch the bias strip to the quilt ⅝ inch from the raw edges. Turn the folded edge of the bias strip to the wrong side of the quilt, and slipstitch the bias strip in place (*see Stitch Guide, page 146*).

ANYTHING GOES PATCHWORK

Early patchwork quilt makers were fond of the simple, rectangular-patch patterns because they could accommodate virtually any color, type or size of fabric. Even though the patchwork developed more for practical reasons than for beauty, the crafters surely didn't want their creations to be unsightly. Patterns that used dozens of different fabrics allowed the blending of plain and fancy fabrics for an overall attractive effect.

One of the most popular early patterns—called Hit and Miss—was made up of hundreds of tiny fabric rectangles sewn together along their long sides and then pieced together in strips. The pattern was completely random, and the results often were quite quirky and colorful.

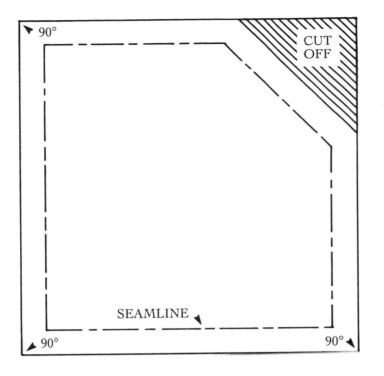

90°

CUT
OFF

90° SEAMLINE 90°

FIG. I, 4A
PATCH PATTERN
FULL SIZE

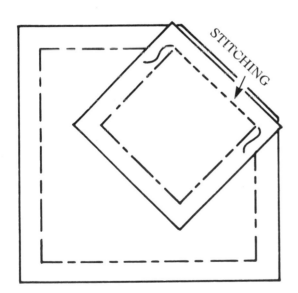

STITCHING

FIG. I, 4B
BOW TIE PATCH ASSEMBLY

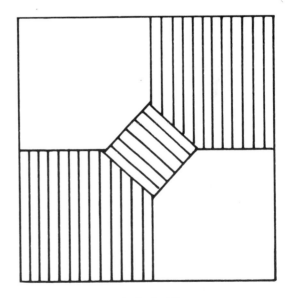

FIG. I, 4C
QUILT BLOCK ASSEMBLY

VICTORIAN CRAZY QUILT

AVERAGE:
For those with some experience in quilting.

DIMENSIONS:
About 54 x 72",
not including ruffle

MATERIALS:
- 5¼ yards of 50-inch-wide pale blue moire for quilt back, ruffle and patches
- 4 yards of assorted fabric scraps including plain and printed velveteens, fine-wale corduroy, moire and taffeta
- 57 x 75-inch piece of synthetic batting
- white sewing thread
- 24 skeins of No. 5 pearl cotton embroidery thread in a variety of colors
- No. 5 pearl cotton embroidery thread: 2 skeins of Pale Blue, 1 skein each of Royal Blue, Yellow, Orange and Light Gold
- embroidery hoop
- embroidery needle
- dressmaker's carbon
- crisp cardboard or manila folder
- tracing paper
- dry ballpoint pen
- Basic Quilting Tools, page 137

We tend to think of crazy quilts as almost overly elegant; representative of the Victorian taste for the opulent. But that wasn't always the case. The oldest crazy quilts were the humblest form of piecework. The first settlers in America had little access to cloth; every scrap of fabric was precious. It didn't make sense to these practical pioneers to cut valuable pieces of cloth into uniform shapes just to make a bedcover, so they would stitch together a haphazard, "crazy" arrangement of patches to produce their quilts.

With the advent of the Victorian era, the growing awareness of foreign cultures, particularly the exotic Orient, and the easy availability of rich fabrics, led to the development of the jewel-toned, heavily embroidered crazy quilts we know today. Victorian quilters favored elaborate, almost fantastical designs, resembling stained glass windows or the patterns seen through kaleidoscopes. Crazy quilts were visual confections of silks and velvets, beads, spangles and embroidery. No proper parlor was complete without a crazy quilt draped over the sofa.

DIRECTIONS:
(¼-inch seams allowed, except where noted)

Note: *An embroidery hoop must be used to embroider this quilt, but remove the fabric from the hoop as soon as you stop working to avoid ring marks on the velveteens.*

1. Pattern: Trace the five full-size patch patterns in FIG. I, 5A *(page 20)* onto tracing paper, making a separate pattern for each patch. Transfer the patch patterns to the crisp cardboard or manila folder, and cut out the patch patterns ¼ inch beyond the traced lines. Number each patch pattern as in FIG. I, 5A.

2. Cutting: From the pale blue moire, cut ten 6 x 50-inch ruffle strips from selvage to selvage, and two 57 x 38-inch pieces for the quilt back. **From the assorted fabrics,** cut out 108 patches each of the five patch patterns for a total of 540 patches.

3. Assembly: Stitch together five of the patches following the diagram in FIG. I, 5A to make a quilt block. The quilt block will be about 6½ inches square. Repeat to make a total of 108 quilt blocks. Place nine quilt blocks in a row, turning the blocks in various directions to mix the colors well and make a pleasing arrangement. Stitch together the quilt blocks, matching the edges of the blocks. Repeat to make 12 rows of quilt blocks. Stitch together four quilt block rows along the long edges; repeat to make three 4-row sections of the quilt top. Because of the weight of the fabric, the quilt is embroidered in sections, then the sections are joined to complete the quilt top.

4. Embroidery: Select a color of thread to contrast with the color of a patch. Work a decorative embroidery stitch across the patch seam in the contrasting thread *(see Stitch Guide, page 146)*. The thread colors and embroidery stitches are the choice of the quilter. Continue to stitch until all the patch seams are covered with embroidery. Stitch together the three quilt top sections along their long edges. Embroider over the patch seams along the long seam lines. Trace the full-size bird pattern in FIG. I, 5B *(page 21)* onto tracing paper. Using the dressmaker's carbon and the dry ballpoint pen, transfer the bird pattern to one corner of the quilt.

(Continued on page 20)

VICTORIAN CRAZY QUILT

VICTORIAN CRAZY QUILT

Embroider the bird, working the wings and body in Royal Blue chain stitch. Work the feathers in Pale Blue feather stitch, working from the tip of the feather toward the body. Work beak in Yellow satin stitch, and eye in an Orange French knot. Outline bird in Light Gold using a small backstitch (*see Stitch Guide, page 146*).

5. Basting: Using a ½-inch seam allowance, stitch together the blue moire quilt back pieces along their long edges. Spread the quilt back, wrong side up, on a clean, flat surface, and tape down the corners. Place the batting and the quilt top, centered and right side up, on top of the quilt back. Starting at the center of the quilt, working straight out to each edge and diagonally out to each corner, baste through all three layers using long stitches;

the basting should stop about 1 inch from the outside edges of the quilt. Add more rows of basting about 10 inches apart, working both vertical and horizontal rows. Trim the quilt back and batting flush with the quilt top. Remove the tape.

6. Tie Quilting: Use a curved or darner needle; a curved needle will make the stitching easier. Thread the needle with a length of the Pale Blue embroidery thread; do not knot the thread. Starting at the center of the quilt, and working from the top, take a short stitch through all three layers at the corner of a quilt block; leave a 2-inch tail of thread. Take another stitch on top of the first. Cut the thread about 2 inches above the stitches. Tie the thread tails into a square knot (*see How To Tie A Square Knot, page 145*), and trim the ends

FIG. I, 5A QUILT BLOCK FULL SIZE

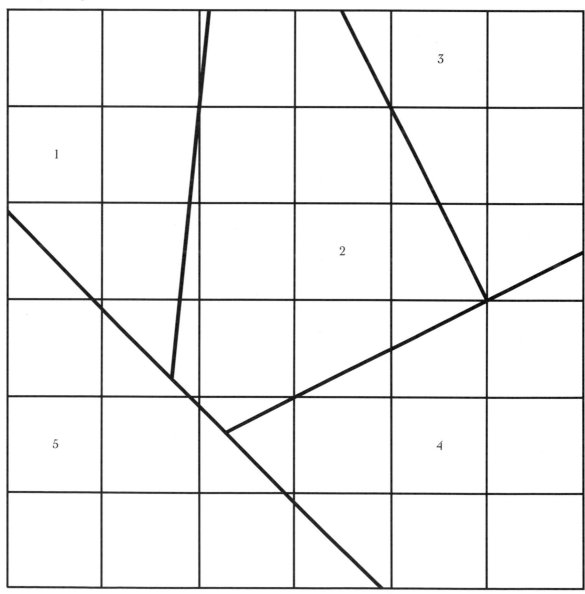

to ½ inch. Repeat across the quilt, making ties at each corner of all the quilt blocks.

7. Ruffle: Stitch together the short ends of the ten ruffle strips to make a long loop. Stitch a narrow hem along one edge. Machine-baste two gathering rows on the opposite long edge, basting ¼ inch and ½ inch from the raw edge; stop and start a new row at each seam to make gathering easier. Pin the ruffle to the quilt, right sides together, matching a ruffle seam to each corner of the quilt. Pin the ruffle so that three sections are on each long side of the quilt, and 2 sections are at the top and bottom. Gather the ruffle to fit the edge of the quilt, distributing the fullness evenly. Machine-stitch the ruffle to the quilt top and batting only; do not catch in the quilt back. Press the seam allowances toward the center of the quilt. Turn under the raw edges of the quilt back, and slipstitch the quilt back to the wrong side of the ruffle, using the gathering row as a stitchline (*see Stitch Guide, page 146*). Remove the basting threads.

FIG. I, 5B
BIRD
FULL SIZE

CRAZY STITCH

Crazy quilts are famous for their luscious array of fancy fabric patches, but they were also used to showcase the stitcher's skills. As if the random combination of fabrics weren't "crazy" enough, all the seams were then embellished with fancy embroidery stitches. But the stitching didn't stop there! It was very common for the quilter to embroider small motifs on the patches. For example, our Victorian Crazy Quilt (*page 18*) features a flying bird on one of its corners. Try personalizing your own quilt by adding special touches like embroidering your family's name, special dates and stitching in scraps of beautiful ribbon and lace. Use the Stitch Guide (*page 146*) for a quick reference on a variety of stitches.

AMISH ROMAN STRIPE QUILT

AVERAGE:
For those with some experience in quilting.

DIMENSIONS:
About 95 x 107″

MATERIALS:
- 45-inch-wide colorfast cotton: 8¾ yards of yellow; 6½ yards of black; 1½ yards each of turquoise, dark red, purple and green
- synthetic batting, pieced as needed to measure 102 x 104 inches
- matching sewing threads
- black or white quilting thread
- crisp cardboard or manila folder
- sharp white dressmaker's pencil
- quilting frame or hoop
- Basic Quilting Tools, page 137

Amish quilts are easily recognized by their juxtaposition of brilliantly colored patches against a dark background. Most Amish quilts are pieced—not appliquéd—in the designs based on traditional, geometric patterns. The quilting patterns vary from simple to highly elaborate.

Our Roman Stripe Quilt is a variation on the traditional Roman Stripe pattern. The stripes are set at an angle instead of in vertical or horizontal blocks as shown in the Roman Square Quilt on page 10. The diagonal stripes of bright color are thought to represent streaks of lightning in the night sky. Sometimes quilters insert one strip of slightly brighter or more intense color in the piecing. This "sparkle" strip, as it's called, makes the lightning image even more apparent.

The quilting on the black patches and side borders echoes the lines of the patch stripes for a harmonious effect. The Amish are not permitted to use printed fabric, however their color choices are not restricted. The results: stunningly simple, extraordinarily beautiful quilts. Traditionally, Amish quilts are stitched only with black or white thread.

DIRECTIONS:

(¼-inch seams allowed, except where noted)

1. Pattern: Draw a right triangle with 12¾-inch-long legs on the cardboard or manila folder; the pattern includes the seam allowance. Use a T-square or drafting triangle to be sure the angle is exactly 90°.

2. Cutting: From the yellow fabric, cut two 45 x 102-inch and one 30 x 102-inch quilt back pieces, cut two 3½ x 90-inch and one 3½ x 60-inch border pieces. **From the black fabric,** cut two 21 x 90-inch and one 21 x 100-inch quilt side pieces, and fourteen 12¾-inch squares. Cut the squares in half diagonally to make 28 right triangles. **From the remaining four fabrics,** cut seven 2⅝ x 45-inch strips.

3. Striped Triangle Patches: Place four of the fabric strips side by side following FIG. I, 6. Keeping the strip ends flush at one end, stitch together the strips along their long edges. Repeat to make a total of seven pieced rectangles. Press all the seams in one direction. Using the cardboard pattern and the dressmaker's pencil, trace four triangles onto each rectangle (*see* FIG. I, 6). Repeat on the remaining rectangles to make a total of 28 striped triangle patches, and cut out the patches.

4. Quilt Block: Stitch a black triangle to a striped triangle patch along their long edges; press the seam toward the black fabric. Repeat to make a total of 28 quilt blocks; half will begin with a green corner and half with a turquoise corner.

5. Assembly: Stitch together four alternating quilt blocks starting with a turquoise corner block (*see photo*). Repeat to make three more rows starting with a turquoise block. Stitch together the remaining quilt blocks in the same way, starting the remaining rows with a green corner block. Starting with a turquoise block row and alternating the rows, stitch together the rows along their long edges.

6. Border: Stitch a long yellow border to the quilt top along a long edge. Repeat on the other long edge of the quilt top. Trim the yellow border ends flush with the quilt top. Stitch the short yellow border to the bottom edge of the quilt top, and trim the border ends flush with the yellow border side edges. Stitch the 90-inch black side borders to the yellow borders, trimming the bottom edges flush with the yellow bottom border. Stitch the 100-inch black

FIG. I, 6
STRIPED TRIANGLE
PATCH PLACEMENT

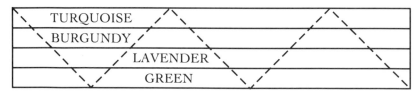

TURQUOISE
BURGUNDY
LAVENDER
GREEN

border to the yellow bottom border, and the short edges of the black side borders.

7. Quilt Back: Cut off the selvages on the yellow quilt back pieces. Using a ½-inch seam and placing the 30-inch-wide piece in the center, stitch together quilt back pieces along the long edges. The quilt back should measure 102 x 118 inches.

8. Basting: If the batting needs to be pieced, spread the pieces on a clean, flat surface with the long edges abutted. Work long cross stitches from one batting piece to the other. The batting should measure approximately 98 x 113 inches. Spread the quilt back, wrong side up, on a clean, flat surface, and tape down the corners. Place the batting, centered, on top of the quilt back. Place quilt top on top of batting, right side up, centered between side edges and 2 inches below top edge of batting. Starting at the center, working straight out to each edge and diagonally out to each corner, baste through the layers using long stitches. Add more rows of basting about

6 inches apart, working both vertical and horizontal rows. Remove the tape.

9. Binding: Trim the batting to 1 inch beyond the top edge of the quilt top, and flush with the black border edges. Trim the yellow quilt back to 1½ inches beyond the black border edges and the top batting edge. Turn under the raw edges of the quilt back ¼ inch. Fold the left edge of the quilt back over the black edge 1¼ inches, and slipstitch the yellow fabric to the quilt top (*see Stitch Guide, page 146*). Repeat on the right-hand side and at the bottom edge of the quilt. Fold the top edge of the quilt back over the batting, and slipstitch the yellow edge in place.

10. Quilting: Using a yardstick and the dressmaker's pencil, extend the lines of the colored strip seams across the black triangles. Mark all the black borders with evenly-spaced, parallel diagonal lines. Using black or white quilting thread, quilt along the marked lines, and over all the seamlines. Remove the basting threads.

AMISH ROMAN
STRIPE QUILT

HEARTS & ROSES QUILT

AVERAGE:
For those with some experience in appliqué and patchwork.

DIMENSIONS:
About 80 x 108"

MATERIALS:
- 45-inch-wide calico print fabric:
  4 yards of red;
  1 yard of green;
  ¼ yard of yellow
- 13 yards of white broadcloth
- 7 yards of synthetic batting
- 325-yard spools of sewing thread:
  5 of green, 2 of red, 1 of yellow
- tracing paper
- crisp cardboard or manila folders
- dressmaker's pencil
- Basic Quilting Tools, page 137

A beautifully appropriate gift to make for a special bride, the appliqué design on our Hearts & Roses quilt combines many of the motifs long associated with wedding quilts—flowers, vines and, of course, hearts.

Traditionally, heart motifs were used only for wedding quilts. They were worked into the quilt both with appliqués and in the quilting itself. Vines and wreaths (as shown on the pillow in the photo at right) also were used to symbolize the marriage union.

Our Hearts & Roses Quilt is a variation on the Foundation Rose and Pine Tree quilt patterns, made to be used as a bedspread. The quilt that inspired our Hearts & Roses Quilt is over a hundred years old and, interestingly, was worked on one of the earliest sewing machines. In our version, the pine tree appliqués were transformed into vines. We added strips of bright calico between the appliquéd quilt blocks, although many antique wedding quilts were made from one large piece of fabric, not piecework.

Bridal quilts often were made at quilting bees. Sometimes the bride-to-be would host the event, but in some communities it was considered bad luck for the bride-to-be to work on her own wedding quilt. In that case, the woman's friends would gather together to make the quilt as a gift for the bride.

(Continued on page 26)

HEARTS & ROSES QUILT

HEARTS & ROSES QUILT DIRECTIONS:

(½-inch seams allowed)

1. Pattern: Trace the full-size appliqué half-patterns in Fig. I, 7 *(pages 28-29)* onto folded tracing paper, placing the broken line on the fold. Trace the half-pattern to the other side of the tracing paper, and open the paper for the full pattern. Transfer the flower, calyx, leaf and heart appliqué patterns individually to the crisp cardboard or manila folders to make a separate pattern for each. Label the appliqué patterns following Fig. I, 7. Set aside the tracing paper pattern.

2. Cutting: From white broadcloth, cut fifteen 16-inch squares for the large quilt blocks, eight 5½-inch squares for the small quilt blocks, two 11 x 96-inch side borders, one 11 x 59-inch bottom border and two 109 x 45-inch quilt back pieces. **From red calico,** cut twenty-two 5½ x 16-inch strips, four 3 x 96-inch strips, two 3 x 88-inch strips, two 3 x 11-inch strips and one 3 x 59-inch strip. Using the cardboard patterns, also cut out 15 hearts, 30 center tulip petals and 45 roses. **From green calico,** using the cardboard patterns, cut out 309 leaves and 45 calyxes for the roses. **From yellow calico,** using the cardboard patterns, cut out 30 outer tulip petals.

3. Large Quilt Block: Using the dressmaker's pencil and the tracing paper pattern, and referring to the photo on pages 24-25 as a placement guide, lightly mark the flower stems and the positions of the rose and tulip heads, the rose calyxes, the leaves and heart on a large white broadcloth square. Using a machine satin stitch, embroider the stems, stitching over them three or four times. Pin the rose and tulip heads, the rose calyxes, the leaves and heart in place. Using thread to match the appliqués, hand-baste them to the large white square, stitching as close to the appliqué edges as possible. Using a machine satin stitch and matching threads, sew around all the appliqué edges twice. Repeat to make a total of 15 large appliquéd quilt blocks.

4. Small Quilt Block: Using one of the cardboard leaf patterns, the dressmaker's pencil, and the photo as a placement guide, lightly mark the positions of the four leaves on the small white broadcloth square. Pin four leaf appliqués over the marked leaves. Using matching thread, hand-baste the leaf appliqués to the small white square, stitching as close to the appliqué edges as possible. Using a machine satin stitch and matching thread, sew around the appliqué leaves twice. Repeat to make a total of 8 small appliquéd quilt blocks.

5. Assembly: Stitch together a row of five large quilt blocks, with the top rose on each block pointing to the top of the quilt, alternating the blocks with 5½ x 16-inch strips of red calico. Repeat to make two more rows of five large quilt blocks and red calico strips. Trim the short ends of the red calico strips flush with the edges of the quilt blocks. Stitch a row of small quilt blocks alternating with the remaining 5½ x 16-inch red calico strips, beginning and ending the row with a red calico strip and joining the strips to the blocks at the short edge. Repeat to make a second row of small quilt blocks and red calico strips. Stitch a small quilt block row to a large quilt block row along the top long edge of the large block row, matching the small quilt block seams to the seams joining the calico strips to the large quilt blocks. Repeat to join the second small block row to the bottom long edge of a second large block row. Stitch both small block rows to the remaining large block row along either long edge, matching the seams as before. Stitch one 3 x 98-inch strip of red calico to each long side of the the quilt block assembly. Trim the ends of the calico strips flush with the quilt block assembly.

6. Borders: Using the dressmaker's pencil and the photo as a guide, draw a wavy line down the center of an 11 x 96-inch white broadcloth border. Repeat on the second border. Using a machine satin stitch, embroider the marked stems on each border, stitching over the stem lines three or four times. Arrange 72 green leaves on each border, placing the leaves on either side of the stem. Hand-baste the leaves in place. Using a machine satin stitch and matching threads, sew around the appliqué leaves twice. Repeat the marking, embroidering and appliqué on the 11 x 59-inch white bottom border, using the remaining 45 leaves. Stitch a side border to the quilt block assembly along a long edge. Repeat with the second side border on the opposite side of the quilt block assembly. Stitch a 3 x 96-inch red calico strip to the long raw edge of a side border. Repeat with the remaining 3 x 96-inch red calico strip on the opposite side border. Trim the ends of the red calico strip flush with short ends of the side borders. Stitch a 3 x 88-inch red calico strip, centered, to the top edge of the quilt block assembly and the extending raw edges of the side borders. Repeat with the second 3 x 88-inch red calico strip at the bottom of the quilt block assembly. Trim the short ends of the red calico strips flush with the outside edges of the side borders. Stitch a 3 x 11-inch red calico strip to either short end of the bottom border. Stitch the bottom border to the bottom edge of the quilt block assembly (the points of the appliqué hearts in the large blocks should point toward the bottom border). Stitch the 3 x 59-inch red calico strip to the long raw edge of the bottom border, and trim the ends flush with the red calico on the bottom border short sides.

7. Quilt Back: Cut the batting into two 3-yard-long pieces. Place the pieces on a clean, flat surface with their long edges abutted. Work long cross stitches from one batting piece to the other. The combined batting should measure approximately 108 x 90 inches. Stitch together the quilt back pieces along a long edge, and press the seam to one side.

8. Basting: Spread the quilt back, right side up, on a clean, flat surface, and tape down the corners. Place the quilt top, centered and wrong side up, on top of the quilt back. Center the batting on top of the quilt top, and pin together all three layers in several places. Trim all the edges, including the quilt back, flush with the quilt top. Remove the tape. Stitch together all three layers around three sides and four corners of the quilt, leaving a 36-inch opening on the top straight edge for turning. Turn the quilt right side out, and slipstitch the opening closed (*see Stitch Guide, page 146*). Starting at the center, working straight out to each edge and diagonally out to each corner, pin-baste through all three layers. Using matching threads, machine quilt on top of all the seamlines. Remove the basting pins.

HEARTS & ROSES PILLOW

DIRECTIONS:

1. Pattern: Make the full traced pattern and appliqué patterns following the directions in Step 1, Heart & Roses Quilt (*page 26*).

2. Cutting: From the white broadcloth, cut one 14-inch square. **From the red calico,** cut one 19-inch square for the pillow back, two 2½ x 14-inch borders and two 2½ x 19-inch borders. Using the appliqué patterns, cut out 4 hearts and 4 tulip center petals. **From the green calico,** using the appliqué pattern, cut out 12 leaves. **From the yellow calico,** using the appliqué pattern, cut out 6 outer tulip petals.

3. Pillow Front: Using the dressmaker's pencil, draw a 7-inch-diameter circle, centered, on the white broadcloth square. Using the photo on pages 24-25 as a guide, machine satin stitch a stem over the marked circle, following the directions in Hearts & Roses Quilt, Step 3 (*page 26*). Place the tulips around the circular stem, equally spaced, and machine appliqué them in place following Step 3. Machine appliqué the green leaves in pairs, one leaf slightly above the other, around the stem. Place the four red hearts with their points toward the corners of the white square, leaving about 1 inch from the sides of the heart point to the edges of the square. Machine appliqué the hearts in place.

4. Pillow Border: Stitch a 2½ x 14-inch red calico border to the opposite sides of the square. Stitch a 2½ x 19-inch red calico border to the remaining raw edges of the square. Press all the seams toward the red fabric.

5. Assembly: Place the appliquéd square, wrong side up, on a clean, flat surface. Place the batting square on top of the appliquéd square, and baste them together. Place the red calico pillow back, right side up, on a flat surface. Place the pillow front with the attached batting, right side down and centered, on top of the pillow back. Stitch around three sides and four corners of the pillow cover, leaving an opening on one edge for turning. Turn the pillow cover right side out, and stuff the pillow firmly. Slipstitch the opening closed.

AVERAGE: For those with some experience in appliqué and patchwork.

DIMENSIONS: About 19″ square

MATERIALS:
- ⅔ yard of 45-inch-wide red print fabric
- scraps of green print and yellow print fabric
- ½ yard of white broadcloth
- matching sewing threads
- 19-inch-square of synthetic batting
- crisp cardboard or manila folders
- synthetic stuffing
- Basic Quilting Tools, page 137

FIG. I, 7
APPLIQUÉ HALF PATTERN
FULL SIZE

PLACE ON FOLD

R = RED
G = GREEN
Y = YELLOW

NEW LOOKS

THE ART OF QUILT-MAKING CHANGES A LITTLE WITH EACH NEW GENERATION OF STITCHERS. NEW FABRICS, COLORS AND FASHIONS LEAD TO NEW QUILTING STYLES AND HELP TO MAINTAIN THE CRAFT'S VITALITY.

CHAPTER ONE INTRODUCED YOU TO TIME-TESTED PATTERNS, BELOVED FOR GENERATIONS. IN THIS CHAPTER, WE TAKE YOU A STEP BEYOND TRADITION — AND OPEN YOUR EYES TO THE LIMITLESS POTENTIAL OF QUILT-MAKING.

CHAPTER 2

SOME OF THESE QUILTS ARE DIRECT DESCENDANTS OF THE CLASSICS; THE TECHNIQUES USED ARE THE SAME, OR VERY SIMILAR, AND THE FABRICS ARE FAMILIAR. BUT THESE QUILTS EACH DIFFER FROM THE TRADITIONAL IN SOME ESSENTIAL FASHION. SOME USE FAVORITE FABRICS IN UNUSUAL WAYS, SOME INTRODUCE CONTEMPORARY COLORS TO A CLASSICALLY INSPIRED DESIGN. THERE EVEN IS A COLLECTION OF QUILTS SCALED TO HANG ON YOUR WALL AS ART.

THE QUILTS IN THIS CHAPTER OFFER YOU THE OPPORTUNITY TO STRETCH THE BOUNDARIES OF THE KNOWN CRAFT, TO CREATE MODERN DAY CLASSICS.

PLAIN & FANCY STAR QUILT
(directions, page 32)

PLAIN & FANCY STAR QUILT

DIMENSIONS:
About 96 x 112″

MATERIALS:
- 39-inch-wide velvet:
  1½ yards each of red,
  gold, yellow, green,
  lavender and maroon
- 45-inch-wide fabric:
  7½ yards of one or
  more shades of blue
  denim;
  10 yards of blue calico
  for quilt back and
  edge facing
- 9 yards of 45-inch-
  wide bonded
  synthetic batting
- quilting hoop
  or frame
- white quilting thread
- Basic Quilting Tools,
  page 137

A new look at an old design, this colorful quilt combines the classic star motif with a wonderful blend of fabrics. The unexpected pairing of blue denim and brightly colored velvet creates an exciting textural contrast as well as a dazzling display of color.

Our Plain & Fancy Quilt is made one block at a time. First, six matching velvet diamonds are stitched together to make a star. Then six denim diamonds are sewn around the velvet star to complete a hexagonal quilt block. Nine quilt blocks are joined to make one row, and four rows are stitched together to make three sections. Each section is quilted separately, then the three sections are joined to complete the quilt top.

PATCHWORK "RECYCLING"

Patchwork was born of practicality. When the early colonists arrived on our shores, they had to improvise many items of daily life taken for granted back in the old country. Single, large pieces of fabric were much too rare and expensive for colonists to use as bedcovers. So, the resourceful pioneers began piecing together usable scraps of worn clothing and other fabrics to make their quilts. In many ways, patchwork is one of the earliest forms of recycling!

The result was not only economical but truly beautiful. The seemingly random combinations of colors and patterns were an early form of abstract art. No two quilts were exactly alike.

Of course, the primary function of quilts was to keep the family warm. And long after America's colonial days, patchwork was popular among the brave and thrifty settlers of the west.

GENERAL CUTTING DIRECTIONS:

1. Marking diamond patches: Gently pull the velvet and denim until their ends are straightened. Working across the width of the fabric, and using the dressmaker's pencil, lightly draw parallel lines 3½ inches apart down the length of the fabric (*see* FIG. II, 1A). Starting at the top left selvage edge, mark off every 4 inches across the top edge of the fabric. On the first drawn horizontal line, measure 2 inches in from the selvage edge of the fabric, then mark off every 4 inches. Mark the second drawn horizontal line every 4 inches, beginning at the fabric edge. Mark the third row, and all odd rows as for the first row. Mark the even rows as for the second row. Continue marking the horizontal lines to make 13 velvet rows and 64 denim rows.

2. Cutting: Using a yardstick, connect all the marks on the horizontal lines with parallel diagonal lines (*see* FIG. II, 1A). Cut out the diamond patches.

3. For denim only: Discard the triangular fabric scraps left at both ends of each horizontal strip after cutting out the diamond patches (*see shaded section in* FIG. II, 1A, *Detail*). From the remaining incomplete diamond shapes, draw half-diamonds as follows: Draw the seamline from right to left between the two opposite points (*the broken line in* FIG. II, 1A, *Detail*). Measure ¼ inch beyond the first line, and draw a cutting line (*the heavy line in* FIG. II, 1A, *Detail*). Cut out the half-diamond. You will need two half-diamonds to complete each half quilt block for a total of 24 half-diamonds.

DIRECTIONS:
(¼-inch seams allowed)
Note: When joining the diamond patches, begin and end stitching ¼ inch from the end of each seamline.

1. Cutting: From denim, cut 636 diamond patches and 24 half-diamonds. **From velvet,** cut 108 diamond patches from each of the six colors. **From blue calico,** cut three 45 x 102-inch quilt back pieces, and 2-inch-wide bias strips, pieced together to make 15 yards of binding.

2. Patchwork Stars: Each star is made up of six velvet diamonds of the same color. Stitch together two velvet diamonds along one edge. Stitch a third diamond to the opposite edge of one of the joined diamond patches to make a half-star. Repeat with three more diamonds to make a second half-star. Stitch together the two half-stars, matching the seams in the center to complete a star. Repeat to make 18 stars of each color. Set aside six gold and six maroon half-stars.

3. Quilt Block: Pin a denim diamond patch between each point of a velvet star (*see* FIG. II, 1B, *page 34*). Stitch the denim diamonds to the star points, pivoting the fabric at the inside point of the star, to make a hexagonal quilt block. Repeat with the remaining denim diamonds and velvet stars to make 102 quilt blocks: 18 each of red, yellow, lavender and green, and 15 each of gold and maroon. Using the remaining denim diamond patches, the denim half-diamonds and the reserved gold and maroon half-stars, make six gold half quilt blocks and six maroon half quilt blocks.

4. Assembly: Follow the Quilt Block Assembly Diagram in FIG. II, 1B for the color and order of the quilt block rows. Stitch together nine quilt blocks to make Row 1. Repeat to make two more Row 1's. Stitch together nine more quilt blocks to make a Row 3. Repeat to make two more Row 3's. Stitch together eight quilt blocks with a half quilt block at each end to make Row 2. Repeat to make two more Row 2's. Stitch together eight more quilt blocks with a half quilt block at each end to make Row 4. Repeat to make two more Row 4's. Following the Assembly Diagram, stitch together four quilt block rows to make a panel. Repeat to make two more panels.

5. Basting: Spread out one quilt back piece, wrong side up, on a clean, flat surface, and tape down the corners. Place a piece of batting the same size on top of the quilt back piece. Center one pieced quilt top panel, right side up, on top of the batting. Starting at the center, working straight out to each edge and diagonally out to each corner, baste through all three layers using long stitches. Add more rows of basting about 4 to 6 inches apart, working both vertical and horizontal rows. Repeat with the remaining quilt back pieces, batting and pieced quilt top panels.

6. Quilting: Place one basted panel in a quilting hoop or frame. Start quilting from the center and work outward. Thread a quilting needle with quilting thread, and tie a knot at one end. Insert the needle into the back of the quilt through the quilt top. Pull the knot up into the batting with a quick, firm tug. Quilt, using small

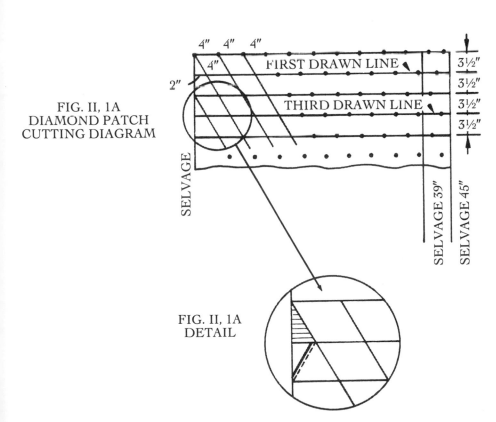

FIG. II, 1A
DIAMOND PATCH
CUTTING DIAGRAM

FIG. II, 1A
DETAIL

FIG. II, 1B QUILT BLOCK ASSEMBLY DIAGRAM

TOP CORNER

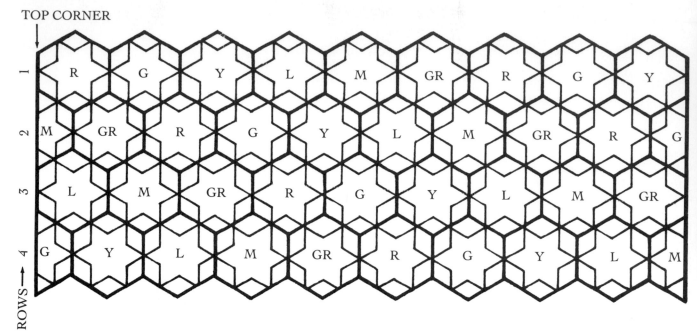

ROWS →

G = GOLD
GR = GREEN
L = LAVENDER
M = MAROON
R = RED
Y = YELLOW

running stitches through all three layers, about ¼ inch from all the seamlines. As a section is completed, remove the hoop immediately to avoid making rings in the velvet. Do not quilt the denim patches along the outside edges of the panels.

7. Joining: Pin together two quilted panels along their long, jagged edges, pinning only through the quilt top. Stitch the panels together through the quilt top only, pivoting the quilt blocks at each point to insure a snug fit. Spread out the quilt face down. Working through the open quilt back, trim the batting edges until they just butt and the quilt lays flat. Trim two raw quilt back edges so one edge overlaps another by 1 inch. Turn under the overlapping raw edge and slipstitch the overlap to the other quilt back piece (*see Stitch Guide, page 146*). Repeat to join the third quilted panel. Remove the basting threads.

8. Finishing: Turn the quilt right side up, and quilt about ¼ inch from the denim seams and over the panel joining seams. Trim the batting and quilt back along their outside edges flush with the quilt top.

9. Binding: Stitch a binding strip to a long edge of the quilt top, right sides together and edges matching. Trim the ends of the binding flush with the quilt. Turn under the raw edge, fold the binding to the quilt back, and slipstitch the binding in place. Repeat on the other long edge of the quilt. Stitch a binding strip to the top edge of the quilt, right sides together and edges matching, with the binding ends extending 1 inch beyond the quilt sides. Turn under the raw edge and fold the binding to the quilt back. Clip the inside corners and miter the binding at the outside corners. Turn under the raw binding edges and slipstitch the binding in place. Repeat on the quilt's bottom edge.

COUNTRY APPLES QUILT

Few sights are as evocative of "country" as an orchard full of crisp red apples. The Country Apples Quilt (directions, page 36) captures that charm with its jaunty apple appliqués and bright, bold colors. To finish the set, make the matching throw pillows and bolsters.

All of the apple appliqués in this quilt are made in the same way. To create the apple halves, simply appliqué a second layer on top of the first. Although the Country Apples Quilt uses red apples, this quilt also can be made with Granny Smith green apples, Golden Delicious yellow apples, or a mixture of all three apples. The placement of whole and half apples is completely random.

COUNTRY APPLES QUILT DIRECTIONS:

(½-inch seams allowed, except where noted)

1. Patterns: Trace the full-size apple patterns in FIG. II, 2A onto the cardboard or manila folders, making a separate pattern for each part of the apple *(see heavy lines in* FIG. II, 2A). Label and cut out the patterns. Trace the complete pattern in FIG. II, 2A onto another piece of cardboard, adding the broken lines; this is the quilting pattern for the quilt blocks.

2. Cutting: From the white fabric, cut ninety 9-inch square blocks. **From the green fabric,** cut ten 3 x 103-inch strips and ninety-nine 3 x 9-inch strips. **From the red fabric,** cut four 7 x 105-inch strips for quilt binding. **From the calico,** cut two 28 x 108-inch quilt back pieces, and one 44 x 108-inch quilt back piece.

3. Apple Appliqués: Trace each of the apple pattern pieces separately onto the right side of the fabric needed, leaving ½ inch between each piece. Cut out the appliqué pieces ¼ inch beyond the traced lines. Trace and cut out the following appliqué pieces: **From the red fabric,** 90 whole apples. **From the green fabric,** 90 stems and leaves, and 56 seeds. **From the white fabric,** 56 apple cross-sections. Flop the pattern over for about half of the green stems.

4. Quilt Block: Pin a red apple to a white square, centered and about ¾ inch from the bottom of the square. Insert a stem between the apple and the square at the indentation so the stem end is about 1 inch below the top of the apple, and pin the stem in place. Turn under the side and top edges of the stem, and slipstitch the stem in place *(see Stitch Guide, page 146)*; when turning under the raw edges of the appliqués, the traced lines will form the finished edges. Turn under the raw edges of the apple, and slipstitch in place. Pin a leaf so that one point just touches the stem, turn under the raw edges and slipstitch it in place. Repeat with the remaining whole red apples, green stems and leaves to complete 89 more quilt blocks, varying stem direction and leaf placement *(see photo, page 35)*. Slipstitch white cross-sections and seeds to 28 quilt blocks, placing the cross-sections and seeds on top of the whole apples. Place the quilt blocks face down, and press.

5. Quilt Top Assembly: Arrange the quilt blocks in nine vertical rows of ten blocks each, inserting the blocks with the half apples randomly in the arrangement. Stitch a 3 x 9-inch green strip to the top edge of a quilt block, right sides together and raw edges matching. Repeat at the bottom edge of the quilt block. Stitch a second quilt block top edge to the bottom of the second green strip. Continue to stitch green strips between quilt blocks until you have completed a vertical row of 10 quilt blocks and 11 green strips *(see FIG. II, 2B, page 38, and photo, page 35)*. Press the seams toward the green fabric. Repeat to make eight more vertical quilt block rows. Fold a vertical row in half crosswise with right sides together, and mark the fold. Fold the row in half again and mark the quarter folds. Repeat with the remaining vertical quilt block rows. Fold a 3 x 103-inch green strip in half crosswise and mark the fold. Fold the strip in half again and mark the quarter folds. Repeat for the remaining long green strips. Stitch together a long green strip to the left side of a vertical quilt block row, right sides together, matching the fold marks and raw edges. Continue to stitch long green strips on either side of the vertical quilt block rows until the quilt top is complete (nine quilt block rows and ten long green strips). Press the seams toward the green fabric.

6. Quilt Back: Stitch together the three calico quilt back pieces along their long edges, placing the wider piece in the center. Press the seams to one side.

7. Basting: To piece together the batting, spread the pieces on a clean, flat surface with their edges abutted. Work long cross stitches from one batting piece to the other. Place the quilt back, right side down, on a clean, flat surface, and tape down the corners. Place the batting on top of the quilt back, and trim the batting flush with edges of the quilt back. Place the quilt top, right side up and centered, on top of the batting; the batting/quilt back will extend 3 inches beyond all four edges of the quilt top. Gently pull the quilt top until the seamlines are squared. Starting at the center, working straight out to each edge and diagonally out to each corner, baste through all three layers using

(Continued on page 38)

AVERAGE:
For those with some experience in quilting.

DIMENSIONS:
About 98 x 108″

MATERIALS:
- 45-inch-wide fabrics: 6 yards each of white, green and red cotton or polyester/cotton, selvage edges removed; 9 yards of red or green calico, selvage edges removed
- matching sewing threads
- matching quilting threads
- two pieces of 90 x 108-inch synthetic batting
- white and blue vanishing-type dressmaker's pencils
- crisp cardboard or manila folders
- quilting hoop or frame
- Basic Quilting Tools, page 137

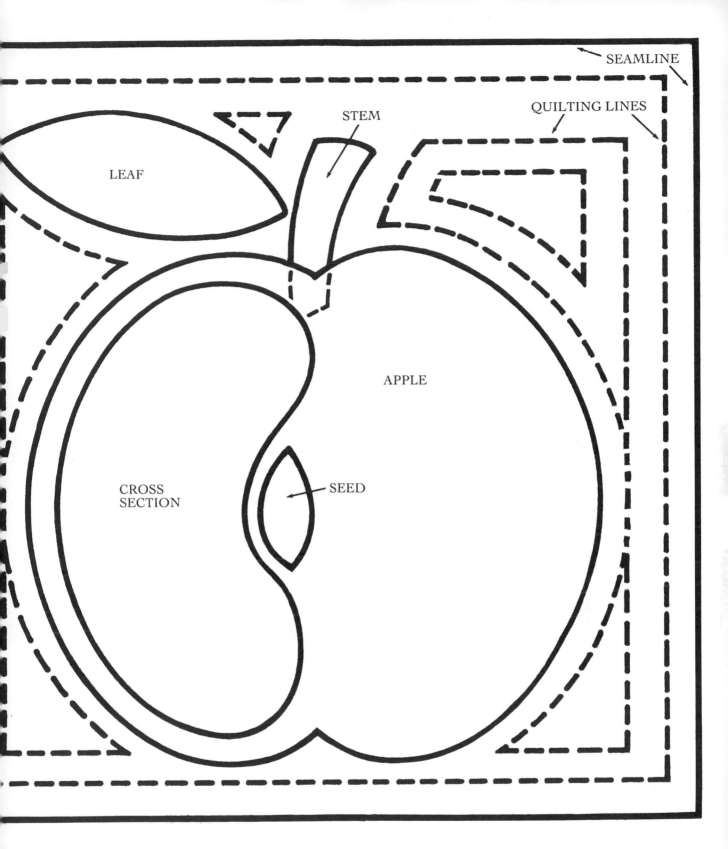

SEAMLINE

QUILTING LINES

STEM

LEAF

APPLE

CROSS
SECTION

SEED

FIG. II, 2A
APPLE APPLIQUÉ PATTERN
FULL SIZE

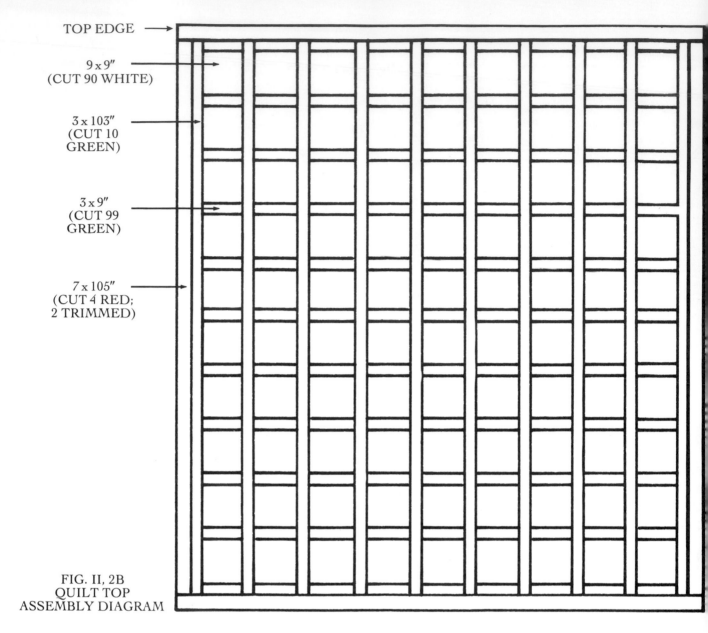

TOP EDGE

9 x 9"
(CUT 90 WHITE)

3 x 103"
(CUT 10
GREEN)

3 x 9"
(CUT 99
GREEN)

7 x 105"
(CUT 4 RED;
2 TRIMMED)

FIG. II, 2B
QUILT TOP
ASSEMBLY DIAGRAM

long stitches. Add more rows of basting about 6 inches apart, working both vertical and horizontal rows. Remove the tape.

8. Quilting: Place the quilt in a quilting hoop or frame. Start quilting from the center and work outward. Using small running stitches through all three layers, quilt about ⅜ inch from each seam, stitching on both sides of the seam. Quilt around the apple appliqués following the stitch lines in FIG. II, 2A (page 37).

9. Binding: Turn under and press one long edge of all four red binding strips. Fold each strip in half crosswise and mark the center fold. Stitch a binding strip to one long edge of the quilt top, right sides

together and raw edges even; match the center fold mark on the binding strip with the center fold mark on the quilt top side edge. Fold the pressed edge of the binding over the exposed batting to the quilt back, and slipstitch the binding to the quilt back (see Stitch Guide, page 146). Repeat with a second binding strip on the opposite long edge of the quilt top, and with the remaining binding strips at the top and bottom edges of the quilt. Trim the ends of the top and bottom binding strips to 1 inch beyond the quilt side edges. Turn under the strip ends until the folded edge is flush with the side edges of the quilt, and slipstitch the opening closed.

COUNTRY APPLES PILLOW AND BOLSTER

DIRECTIONS:

1. Appliqué: For the pillow, make the patterns, cut out the appliqué pieces and stitch them to the white square following Steps 1, 3 and 4 of Country Apples Quilt (*page 36*). For the bolster, appliqué two white squares.

2. Square Pillow Top: Stitch a 3 x 9-inch green strip to either side of the appliquéd square. Stitch a 3 x 13-inch green strip to the top and bottom edges of the square. Repeat with the red strips, stitching them to the raw edges of the green strips.

Bolster Top: Stitch the two white squares between the three 3 x 9-inch green strips, stitching the strips to the side edges of the squares. Stitch the 3 x 23-inch green strips to the top and bottom edges of the square assembly. Repeat with the red strips, stitching the 2 x 13-inch red strips to the short ends of the assembly, and the 2 x 25-inch red strips to the long top and bottom edges of the assembly. Baste and quilt the pillow and/or bolster tops using the batting pieces and the muslin backing, following Steps 7 and 8 of Country Apples Quilt (*pages 36 and 38*).

3. Assembly: Using ½-inch seams, stitch the pillow top to the pillow back, right sides together and edges even, around three sides and four corners, leaving an opening on one side for turning. Turn the pillow right side out, stuff it and slipstitch the opening closed (*see Stitch Guide, page 146*). Repeat for the bolster.

AVERAGE:
For those with some experience in quilting.

DIMENSIONS:
Pillow, about 14" square; bolster, about 14 x 24"

MATERIALS:

For square pillow:
- one 9-inch white fabric square
- 14-inch muslin square to back quilting
- two 3 x 13-inch and two 3 x 9-inch green fabric strips
- two 2 x 15-inch and two 2 x 13-inch red fabric strips
- one 15-inch red fabric square pillow back
- 15-inch square of synthetic batting

For bolster:
- two 9-inch white fabric squares
- one 15 x 25-inch muslin rectangle to back quilting
- three 3 x 9-inch and two 3 x 23-inch green fabric strips
- two 2 x 13-inch and two 2 x 25-inch red fabric strips
- 15 x 25-inch red fabric pillow back
- 15 x 25-inch piece of synthetic batting

For pillow and bolster:
- scraps of red, green and white fabric for appliqués
- matching quilting thread
- quilting frame or hoop
- synthetic stuffing
- crisp cardboard or manila folder
- Basic Quilting Tools, page 137

 THE ART OF APPLIQUÉ

The history of appliqué is a fascinating one; we could write volumes on this technique alone. The use of fabric patches to create artistic or decorative pieces dates back at least as far as the Middle Ages. Imagine legions of armor-clad crusaders riding off to battle — their banners and flags, horse-blankets and their clothes brilliantly adorned with appliqué work. This technique originated in Europe, where appliqué developed as a decorative art used to beautify church linens and vestments, and to lavishly decorate items for the nobility.

Most early examples of American quilt appliqué work come from the south, where wealthy women could afford to cut valuable fabric to suit their fancy. In the northern states, fabric was expensive and in short supply, so women would patch together quilts from whatever types and colors of fabric they had available.

Appliqué work gave the stitcher a chance to use curved lines and odd shapes in her designs, and the results were understandably more varied and elaborate than patchwork. Even when fabric was easier to come by, appliqué was still usually reserved for fancier quilts. Some of the most beautiful examples of antique appliqué work feature elaborately detailed designs — birds, flowers and vines with curved edges, and many designs that simply couldn't be done with patchwork. Other classic appliqué patterns, such as the Dresden Plate, Grandmother's Fan and the Double Wedding Ring, show a strong patchwork influence.

WATER LILY QUILT

AVERAGE:
For those with some experience in quilting.

MATERIALS:

For Queen-Size Quilt:
- 45-inch-wide cotton calico print:
  4 yards of rust;
  3 yards of blue;
  2 yards of brown
- 1½ yards of muslin for appliqué squares
- 6 yards of permanent press muslin, or a solid color Queen-size flat sheet for quilt back
- 2 packages of Queen-size synthetic batting

For King-Size Quilt (directions, page 43):
- 45-inch-wide cotton calico print:
  4½ yards of rust;
  4 yards of blue;
  3 yards of brown
- 2⅝ yards of muslin for appliqué squares
- 10 yards of permanent press muslin, or a solid color King-size flat sheet, for quilt back
- 2 packages of King-size synthetic batting

For both quilts:
- matching sewing threads
- crisp cardboard or manila folders
- matching 4-ply yarn
- Basic Quilting Tools, page 137

Cotton calicos and a blend of autumnal hues give this appliquéd quilt a traditional look, although the water lily design is quite contemporary. The color shades shown in the photo are similar to those associated with the Colonial period, heightening the classical element of the quilt; however, the colors may be changed to suit a different color scheme or decorative style. For a more contemporary look, substitute ice pink and leaf green, sky blue and lemon yellow, or navy blue and fire-engine red. For a more subtle approach, try several harmonious shades of one color such as pale to forest green or baby yellow to marigold. If you have an artistic eye, try capturing the soft pinks, purples, blues and greens in Claude Monet's paintings of "Water Lilies."

Instead of a running quilting stitch, the Water Lily Quilt is tie-quilted. A simple technique, tie-quilting can be used in just about any quilt project, however tie-quilting can only be done with synthetic batting. Natural fiber batting, such as cotton, tends to bunch up in the wash and requires more stitching to hold it in place.

GENERAL DIRECTIONS:
(⅜-inch seams allowed)

Note: The General Directions given are for a Queen-size quilt. The quilt in the photo is a King-size quilt; the changes for the King-size quilt are on page 43.

1. Pattern: Trace the full-size petal pattern in FIG. II, 3 *(page 42)* onto the crisp cardboard or manila folder, and cut out the petal pattern. Also draw and cut out a 2-inch-diameter circle.

2. Cutting: From the brown calico, cut 96 petals, twelve circles and 5-inch-wide strips pieced together to measure 9 yards. **From the blue calico,** cut 96 petals and 2½-inch-wide strips pieced together to measure 24 yards. **From the rust calico,** cut 96 petals, 4-inch-wide strips pieced together to measure 12 yards and twenty 7½-inch squares. **From the muslin,** cut twelve 13-inch squares.

3. Quilt Block: Using the photo as a guide, and working from the bottom layer upward, pin the petals in place on the muslin squares. Use 8 petals of each color for a total of 24 petals for each water lily. Start with the bottom layer of brown petals, then a layer of rust, blue, and a brown circle on top for the flower center. Using a machine zigzag stitch and working from the center out, appliqué around all the pieces of the flower. Repeat to make a total of 12 appliquéd quilt blocks.

4. Inner Border: Cut the 2½-inch-wide pieced blue strip in half to make two 12-yard strips. Sew a 2½-inch-wide blue strip to either side of the 4-inch-wide rust strip to make a blue-rust-blue inner border strip. Cut the inner border strip into 13-inch-long strips.

5. Quilt Top: Stitch one long blue edge of an inner border strip to one side of an appliquéd quilt block. Stitch one blue edge of a second border strip to the opposite edge of the quilt block. Repeat to make a row of three quilt blocks joined on either side by inner border strips, beginning and ending the row with a border strip. Repeat to make three more quilt block rows. Trim all the short border strip ends flush with the edges of the quilt blocks.

(Continued on page 42)

WATER LILY QUILT AND SHAM

6. Assembly: Stitch a rust square to either short end of an inner border strip. Stitch the short end of a second inner border strip to the opposite side of one of the rust squares. Repeat to make a row of three inner border strips and four rust squares, beginning and ending with a square. Repeat to make four more rows. Stitch a row of inner border strips and rust squares to one long edge of a quilt block row, right sides together and raw edges matching; match the inner border strips to the raw edges of the quilt blocks. Stitch a second inner border row to the opposite long edge of the quilt block row. Repeat until all four quilt block rows are joined by five inner border rows. Stitch a brown outer border strip to one long edge of the quilt block assembly, starting with one short end of the strip flush with the edge of the assembly. Trim the opposite end of the strip flush with the end of the assembly. Repeat on the opposite long edge, and at the top and bottom of the assembly.

7. Basting: If the batting needs to be pieced together, spread the pieces on a clean, flat surface with their edges abutted. Work long cross stitches from one batting piece to the other. Spread the quilt top, wrong side up, on a clean, flat surface, and tape down the corners. Place the batting, centered, on the quilt top, and trim the edges of the batting flush with the edges of the quilt top. Starting at the center, working straight out to each edge and diagonally out to each corner, pin through both layers. Add more rows of pins about 6 inches apart, working both vertical and horizontal rows. Baste through both layers along the pinned lines, removing the pins as you go. Remove the tape. Piece and stitch together the muslin to make a quilt back, or use the sheet for a quilt back; press the seams to one side. Spread the quilt back, right side up, on a clean, flat surface, and tape down the corners. Place the basted quilt top and batting, batting side up and centered, on top of the quilt back; pin all three layers together. Trim the quilt back flush with the quilt top/batting layer. Stitch together all three layers around three sides and four corners, leaving an opening on one side for turning. Turn the quilt right side out, turn in the open edge and slipstitch the opening closed (*see Stitch Guide, page 146*).

8. Tie-Quilting: Spread the quilt, right side up, on a clean, flat surface. Use a curved needle or a darner needle; a curved needle will make the stitching easier. Thread the needle with a length of the yarn; do not knot the yarn. Starting at the center of the quilt, and working from the top, take a short stitch through all three layers at the corner of a quilt block; leave a 2-inch tail of yarn. Take another stitch on top of the first. Cut the yarn about 2 inches above the stitches. Tie the yarn tails into a square knot (*see How To Tie A Square Knot, page 145*), and trim the ends to ½ inch. Repeat across the quilt, making ties every 3 inches on the seamlines.

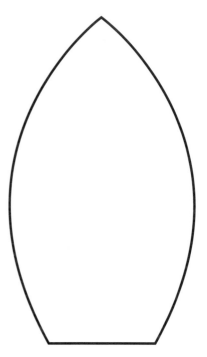

FIG. II, 3
PETAL APPLIQUÉ PATTERN
FULL SIZE

KING-SIZE QUILT DIRECTIONS:

Follow the directions for the Queen-Size Quilt (*pages 40-42*), with the following changes: Cut out 160 petals of each color, twenty 2-inch-diameter brown centers and twenty 13-inch muslin squares. Make 20 appliquéd squares. To make the borders, cut and piece together 18 yards of 4-inch-wide, 36 yards of 2½-inch-wide, and 12 yards of 5-inch-wide brown calico. Stitch together 18 yards of blue-rust-blue inner border strips. The quilt block rows will have 5 appliquéd squares each. Cut thirty 7½-inch squares of rust. The five inner border/rust square rows will have five border strips and six squares each.

VARIATIONS ON A THEME

One of the joys of quilt-making is the endless variety of projects that can be made from one design simply by changing the color or patterns of the fabrics used to make the quilt. Below are some suggestions for possible quilt variations.

• Substitute calicoes for solid color fabrics called for in a project, or solids for calicoes.
• Reverse the placement of light and dark fabric patches.
• Use all pastels or all primary color fabrics for a distinctive look.

Note: If you are substituting fabrics in a project, make a sample block before purchasing fabric for the entire quilt.

WATER LILY SHAM

DIRECTIONS:

1. Pattern: Make a petal pattern and a 2-inch-diameter flower center pattern following Step 1, Water Lily Quilt (*page 40*).

2. Cutting: From the brown calico, cut 8 petals and one flower center. **From the blue calico,** cut 8 petals and 8-inch-wide strips pieced together to measure 7 yards. **From the rust calico,** cut 8 petals and 4-inch-wide strips pieced together to measure 3 yards. **From the muslin,** cut one 24½ x 14½-inch rectangle for the sham front, and two 30 x 16½-inch rectangles for the sham back.

3. Quilt Block: Appliqué the water lily on the muslin sham front following Step 3, Water Lily Quilt (*page 40*).

4. Sham Front: Stitch a rust strip to one short end of the quilt block, and trim the strip end flush with the quilt block edge. Repeat on the opposite short end. Repeat on the long edges of the quilt block, trimming the rust strip ends flush with the outer edges of the rust border. The sham front should be about 20 x 30 inches.

5. Ruffle: Fold the strip of blue calico in half lengthwise to 4 inches, and press the strip. Stitch two gathering rows along the doubled raw edges, and pull the gathers until the ruffle is 3 yards long. Pin the ruffle to the sham front, right sides together and raw edges matching, distributing the gathers evenly around the sham. Stitch the ruffle to the sham front, easing the ruffle around the corners.

6. Sham Back: Make a 1½-inch hem on a short edge of each sham back piece. Stitch one sham back to the sham front, right sides together, raw edges matching and the ruffle toward the center. Repeat with the second sham back; the sham back open hemmed edges will overlap. Turn the sham right side out and insert the pillow through the back opening.

DIMENSIONS:
About 20 x 30", without ruffles

MATERIALS:

(For each sham)

• 45-inch-wide cotton calico print:
  2 yards of blue;
  ½ yard of rust;
  ⅙ yard of brown
• 1½ yards of muslin
• matching sewing threads
• crisp cardboard or manila folder
• pillow
• Basic Quilting Tools, page 137

DIAMOND IN A SQUARE MINI-QUILT

DIMENSIONS:
About 30½" square

MATERIALS:
- 45-inch-wide solid colorfast cotton: ¼ yard each of black and lavender; ½ yard of burgundy; 1¼ yards of turquoise
- 33-inch square of synthetic batting
- black or white quilting thread
- black sewing thread
- white fabric marking pencil
- quilting hoop or frame
- crisp cardboard or manila folder
- Basic Quilting Tools, page 137

This bold geometric is one of the oldest and best known patch patterns used by the Amish in their quilts. The colors used to make the quilt in the photo are authentically Amish—they're the same colors that the Amish people generally use for their clothing. The twist here is in the size of the quilt. The Amish are "plain people," and everything they make must have a practical purpose. Although Amish quilts are beautiful, their primary function was, and is, as a bedcover. Thus an Amish quilt in miniature is a perfect blend of a classic design reinvented for contemporary usage.

Traditionally, Amish quilting is done only with black or white thread. The piecework in Amish quilts generally is very simple, but the quilting designs often are quite elaborate. Diamond in a Square is often quilted with an intricate circular motif in the center diamond, and then a simpler adaptation of the central motif on the border pieces. The quilt in the photo is stitched with a very simple quilted motif, but a fancier pattern may be easily substituted.

DIRECTIONS:
(¼-inch seams allowed)

Note: Cut all the patches on the grain of the fabric. To make matching triangles, cut a square in half along the diagonal. When piecing the quilt block, pin together the patches at both ends of the seamline, then add additional pins in between the first pins; the raw edges will not match, but the seamlines will. Be sure to stitch exactly ¼-inch from the raw edges. Press all the seams toward the darker fabric.

1. Pattern: Draw a triangle on the crisp cardboard or manila folder using the dimensions in Fig. II, 4 *(page 46)*, making sure the right angle is 90°. Cut out the triangle pattern; the pattern includes the ¼-inch seam allowance.

2. Cutting: From the turquoise fabric, cut one 33-inch square and, using the pattern, four triangles. **From the black fabric,** cut one 7¾-inch square, four 5½-inch squares and four 2½-inch squares. **From the lavender fabric,** cut four 2½ x 16½-inch rectangles and four 2½ x 7¾-inch rectangles. **From the burgundy fabric,** cut four 5½ x 20½-inch rectangles and four 2½-inch squares.

3. Diamond Block: Stitch the long edge of a 7¾-inch lavender rectangle to an edge of the large black square. Repeat on the opposite edge of the square. Stitch a burgundy square to each short end of the remaining two 7¾-inch lavender rectangles, and stitch the strips to the raw edges of the black square and the extending lavender borders.

4. Square Block: Pin the long edge of a turquoise triangle, centered, to one edge of the diamond block. Stitch, beginning and ending ¼ inch from the raw edges. Repeat with the remaining triangles at the raw edges of the diamond block. Following the directions in Step 3, stitch a border of the 16½-inch lavender strips and the small black squares to the turquoise square.

5. Borders: Stitch a long edge of a burgundy rectangle to a raw edge of the square block. Repeat on the opposite edge of the square block. Stitch a 5½-inch black square to each short end of the remaining burgundy rectangles, and stitch the strips to the raw edges of the square block and the extending burgundy borders.

(Continued on page 46)

DIAMOND IN A SQUARE MINI-QUILT

AMISH QUILTING

It seems ironic that the "plain" people, who live so quietly without material or worldly concerns, should create such bold and beautiful quilts. Amish quilts are instantly recognizable both for their striking colors and exquisite stitching.

The patchwork patterns favored by the Amish are often very simple, and almost exclusively pieced with solid color fabrics. All the colors used in the work must be approved by the church, and they tend to run toward darker shades—red, purple, royal blue and black.

Although the quilting stitches used by the Amish are arguably the finest known today, they consider quilting to be merely a practical way to hold together the layers of the quilt.

6. Basting: Spread the quilt back (the large turquoise square), wrong side up, on a clean, flat surface, and tape down the corners. Place the batting on top of the quilt back, then place the quilt top, centered and right side up, on top of the batting. Starting at the center, working straight out to each edge and diagonally out to each corner, baste through all three layers using long stitches. Add more rows of basting about 6 inches apart, working both vertical and horizontal rows. Remove the tape.

7. Binding: Trim the batting to extend ⅜ inch beyond the quilt top. Fold the raw edges of the quilt back ¼ inch to the wrong side, and press in place. Fold the pressed edge over the batting until the edge overlaps the quilt top by ¼ inch. Slipstitch the folded quilt back edge to the quilt top (*see Stitch Guide, page 146*), mitering the corners as you stitch.

8. Quilting: Using the dressmaker's pencil and a yardstick, mark both diagonals across the center black square. Starting from the points of the black square, measure 2 inches in along each drawn diagonal line. Connect these marks to draw a square whose sides parallel the edges of the black square. Mark the small black corner squares in the same way. Place the quilt in a quilting hoop or frame. Start quilting, using the black or white quilting thread, working from the center outward. Quilt, using small running stitches through all three layers, over all the marked lines and ¼ inch from each seam. When the quilting is finished, remove the basting threads. If you wish to hang the quilt, make a casing from the same fabric as the quilt back (*see How to Make a Casing, page 145*).

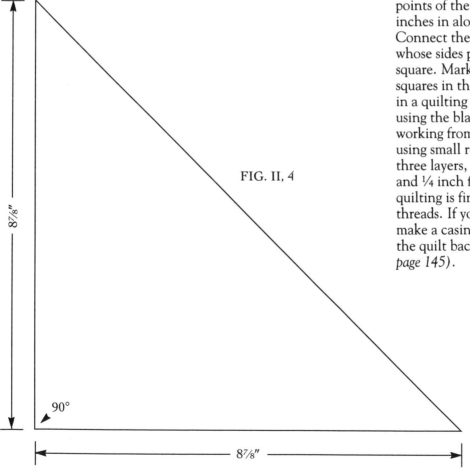

FIG. II, 4

8⅞"

8⅞"

90°

DESERT SUN QUILT

A contemporary quilt with a strong Southwestern influence, the Desert Sun Quilt (directions, page 48) includes rising and setting sun quilting designs derived from motifs found in the artwork of some Native American tribes of the Southwest. The stitching is the primary focus of this quilt, giving texture and adding visual interest to the soft, soothing shades of fabric.

The fabric colors used are gentle earth tones—the colors of sunrise and sunset in the desert. The simplicity of patchwork in this quilt lends itself to many other color choices. There are seven different fabrics used in the quilt; to maintain the subtle color balance, use a slightly darker fabric for the "A" color patch. To create a quilt with greater color contrast, take a cue from handpainted pottery native to the Southwest: black, white, rust, cobalt blue, slate gray, dove gray or sand.

CHALLENGING:
Requires more
experience in quilting.

DIMENSIONS:
About 52 x 56"

MATERIALS:
- 44- to 45-inch-wide
  solid color fabric:
  1 yard of slate gray;
  1½ yards of mauve;
  ¾ yard of dark peach;
  ¼ yard each of
  violet, deep apricot
  and aqua;
  ⅛ yard or scrap of
  pale brick;
  3 yards of solid color
  fabric for quilt back
- ½-inch double fold
  bias binding in color
  to complement or
  match quilt back
- matching quilting
  threads
- 54 x 58-inches
  of synthetic batting
- tracing paper
- crisp cardboard
  or manila folders
- "disappearing" fabric
  marker
- quilting hoop
  or frame
- Basic Quilting Tools,
  page 137

DESERT SUN QUILT DIRECTIONS:

(¼-inch seams allowed)

Note: Fig. II, 5 represents only one-quarter of the quilt top.

1. Patterns: Using the dimensions given, draw the patch patterns *(solid lines)* in Fig. II, 5 onto tracing paper, adding a ¼-inch seam allowance; make a separate pattern for each patch. The patches on the center line are half patterns; to make a whole pattern, fold paper in half, transfer the half pattern, and cut. Open the paper to make full pattern. Transfer patterns to crisp cardboard or manila folders, and cut. On tracing paper patterns, mark all quilting lines *(the dotted lines in Fig. II, 5)* for each patch. Set aside the tracing paper patterns.

2. Cutting: Following the diagram and the color chart in Fig. II, 5, cut out the patches for the quilt top. Cut one of each center panel patch and cut two of each side panel patch. Cut two D borders. Cut the quilt back fabric in half crosswise to make two 1½-yard pieces.

3. Assembly: Following Fig. II, 5, and using the photo on page 47 as a guide, stitch the patches together, beginning and ending the stitching ¼ inch from the raw edges of the patches to allow for seams, and easing corners as needed. Piece together a smaller block of patches, then stitch the patchwork blocks together. The D border strips should be added last to finish the quilt top. Stitch together the quilt back pieces along a long edge.

3. Marking: Using the tracing paper patterns, a ruler, the fabric marker, and Fig. II, 5 as a guide, transfer the quilting lines to the quilt top.

4. Basting: If the batting needs to be pieced together, spread the pieces on a clean, flat surface with their edges abutted. Work long cross stitches from one batting piece to the other. Spread the quilt back, wrong side up, on the clean, flat surface, and tape down the corners. Place the batting on top of the quilt back matching one short edge. Place the quilt top, centered and right side up, on top of the batting. Starting at the center, working straight out to each edge to form a 3- to 4-inch grid pattern, baste through all three layers using very long stitches. Trim the batting and the quilt back to extend 2 to 3 inches beyond the edges of the quilt top. Remove the tape.

5. Quilting: Place the quilt in a quilting hoop or frame. Start quilting from the center and work outward. Use quilting thread that matches each fabric. Quilt, using small running stitches through all three layers, over all marked quilting lines.

6. Binding: When the quilting is finished, trim the batting and quilt back flush with the edges of the quilt top. Pin one folded edge of the bias binding to the quilt top, raw edges matching, mitering the corners as you work. Machine-stitch the bias binding to the quilt top, using the binding fold as a stitch guide. Fold the opposite folded edge of the bias binding over the raw edge of the quilt to the quilt back, and slipstitch the second bias binding fold to the quilt back *(see Stitch Guide, page 146)*. Remove the basting threads. To hang the quilt, make a casing from extra quilt back fabric *(see How to Make a Casing, page 145)*.

CHOOSING A QUILTING PATTERN

The quilting design that completes your quilt is just as important as the color and pieced motif. The pattern of the stitching should enhance the patchwork, and add visual interest to the plain fabric squares or borders. Quilting can be as plain as a simple grid or as elaborate as birds, flowers and shells.

Select a quilting design that best suits the patchwork or appliqué design: A grid pattern for the geometric patchwork of the Bow Tie Quilt *(page 14)*; more elaborate stitching for the Carpenter's Wheel *(page 66)*. Or use the quilting to outline the patchwork or appliqué motifs. Stitch around — never over — the patchwork two to three times.

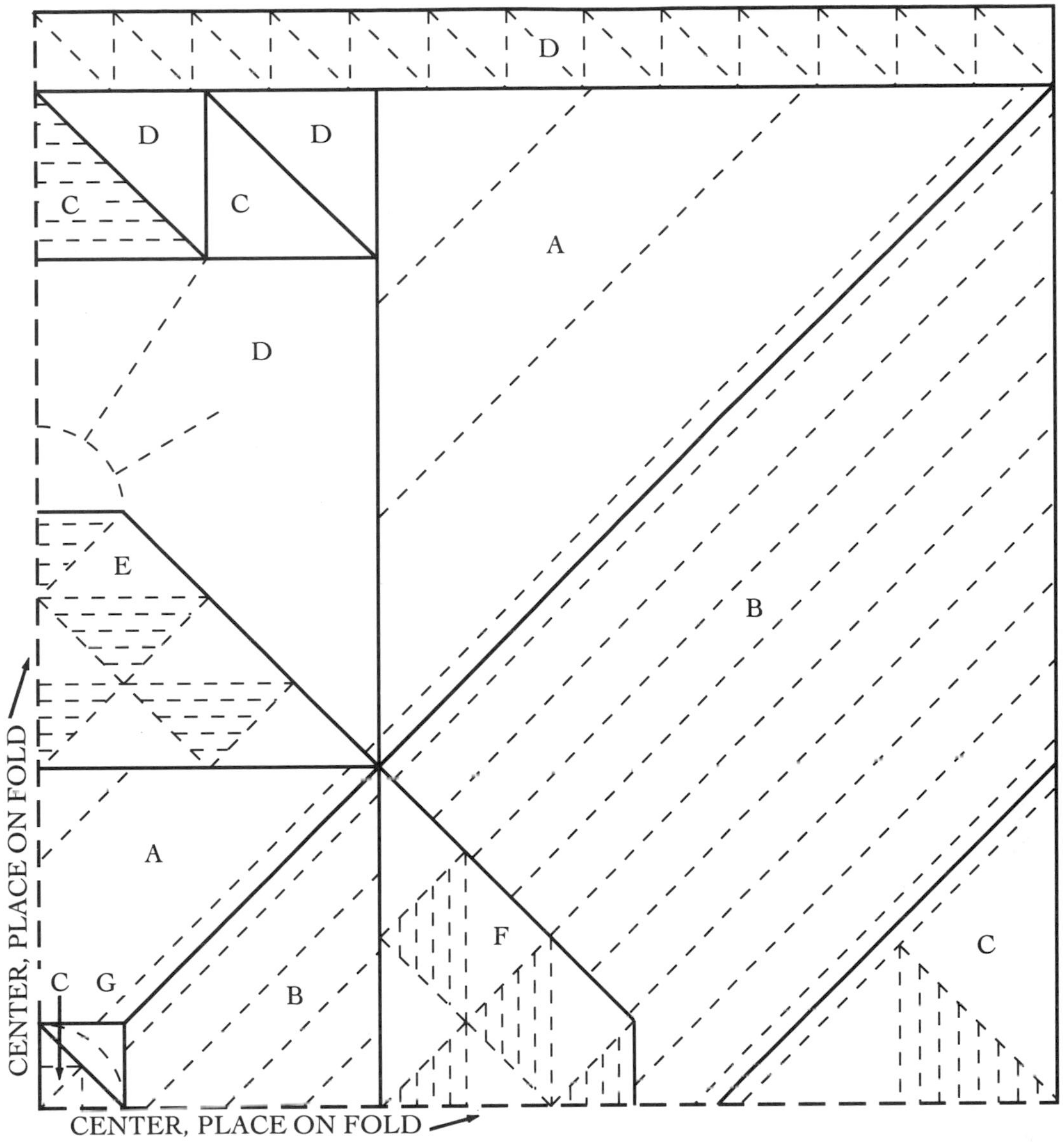
D
D
D
C
C
A
D
E
B
A
F
C
C
G
B
CENTER, PLACE ON FOLD
CENTER, PLACE ON FOLD

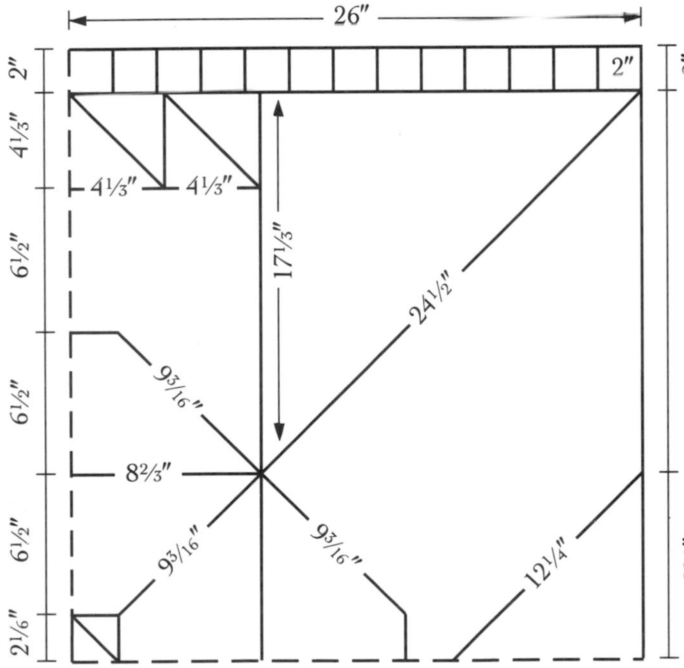
26″
2″
2″
2″
4⅓″
4⅓″
4⅓″
6½″
6½″
6½″
2⅙″
17⅓″
17⅓″
24½″
9³⁄₁₆″
8⅔″
9³⁄₁₆″
9³⁄₁₆″
12¼″
28″
8⅔″
2⅙″
6½″
6½″
2⅙″
8⅔″

FIG. II, 5
PATCH AND QUILTING PATTERN QUARTER-SIZE

A = SLATE GRAY
B = MAUVE
C = VIOLET
D = DARK PEACH
E = DEEP APRICOT
F = AQUA
G = PALE BRICK

SEAMLINES

QUILTING LINES

CAROLINA LILY MINI-QUILT

CHALLENGING:
Requires more experience in quilting.

DIMENSIONS:
About 51″ square

MATERIALS:
- 45-inch-wide cotton fabric:
  3½ yards of green calico;
  ¾ yard of red calico;
  2 yards of solid white;
  1½ yards of solid green
- matching sewing threads
- matching quilting threads
- synthetic batting
- quilting hoop or frame
- crisp cardboard or manila folders
- dressmaker's pencil
- Basic Quilting Tools, page 137

Although many quilt patterns seem to be universally known, often the name of the pattern would vary from place to place. The lily motif, a "cousin" to the LeMoyne Star pattern, is a prime example of regional variation. A favorite of quilters over the years, the lily is found in quilts made both east and west of the Mississippi, from northern New England down to Tennessee. Yet, even though the designs are very similar, the pattern names vary depending on the types of lilies native to a region.

In most Southern states, the pattern was known as the North Carolina Lily, except in Kentucky and Tennessee where it was known as the Mountain Lily. In Pennsylvania, the pattern was known as Tiger Lily. In southern New England it was the Meadow Lily and in northern New England it was the Wood Lily. In Ohio, Indiana and Illinois, the pattern is commonly called Fire Lily, after a native red-flowered weed. In the plains, quilters made Prairie Lily quilts, and farther west the pattern was known as Mariposa Lily.

This version of the Carolina Lily is a classic quilt in miniature — perfect as a gift for a Christmas baby, to hang on the wall or to add a spot of color to any room in the house.

DIRECTIONS:
(¼-inch seams allowed)

1. Patterns: Trace the full-size patterns in Figs. II, 6A and 6C (*page 53*), and the Small Leaf and Large Leaf patterns in Fig. II, 6B (*page 53*) onto crisp cardboard or manila folders. Draw a 3¾-inch square for Patch Pattern B. Label the diamond patch "A," the 3¾-inch square "B" and the triangle "C." Label the two leaf patterns. Cut out all the cardboard patterns.

2. Cutting: To cut a pair of leaves, trace the leaf pattern once, then flop the pattern and trace it a second time to make the opposite leaf. **From the white fabric,** cut two 1½ x 46-inch borders, two 1½ x 48-inch borders, four 1½ x 23-inch strips, four 11½-inch squares, forty-eight B squares, forty-eight C triangles and one 1½-inch square. **From the solid green fabric,** cut two 1¼ x 48-inch borders, two 1¼ x 50-inch borders, four pairs of small leaves and 1½-inch-wide bias strips pieced together to measure about 6 yards. **From the red calico,** cut seventy-two A diamonds. **From the green calico,** cut two 30 x 60-inch quilt back pieces, twenty-four A diamonds and four pairs of large leaves.

3. Flower Block: When stitching together the patches, begin and end the stitching ¼ inch from the raw edges to allow room for joining. Stitch together two red diamonds along one edge, and press the seam to one side. Repeat two times. Stitch together two green diamonds along one edge. Stitch together two of the red pairs along one edge to make a flower half. Stitch together the remaining red pair and the green pair along one edge to make the other half of the flower. Press all the seams to one side. Stitch together the two flower halves, and press the seam open to make a complete flower. Stitch a white B square between the green diamond points, starting from the outer point and stitching toward the center. Stop at the point where the seamlines meet, pivot the assembly, and continue stitching the opposite edges. Repeat between the red petal pair opposite the green assembly. Repeat between the red petal pair to the right and left (*see photo*). Stitch a white C triangle between the four remaining open red diamond petal pairs to complete the flower block. Repeat to make 12 flower blocks.

(Continued on page 52)

CAROLINA LILY MINI-QUILT

When quilting by hand, work with 18-inch lengths of thread to avoid snags and knots.

If you have trouble threading your needle, dab a little hairspray on the end of your thread, or run the thread end over a candle stub or cake of beeswax. This will stiffen the end of the thread and help it glide through the eye of the needle.

4. Quilt Block: Using the photo on page 51 as a guide, stitch together two flower blocks, matching a red and green point on each block. Stitch a third flower block to a large white square. Stitch together the two double blocks, with the white square at the lower right and the green diamonds in the center, to complete the quilt block. Repeat with the remaining flower blocks and large white squares to make three more quilt blocks.

5. Appliqués: Fold the pieced green bias strip in half lengthwise, wrong sides together and long raw edges matching. Stitch down the long edge of the strip ¼ inch from the raw edges. Press the seam open and centered on the back of the strip. Using the photo as a guide, pin the strip diagonally across the quilt block beginning at the bottom of the center flower and ending at the bottom corner of the white square. Turn under the top end of the strip, trimming the excess end. Add two curved stems to the main stem, tucking the ends under the center strip. Slipstitch the stems to the white fabric along all their edges (see Stitch Guide, page 146). Roll under the raw edges of each small leaf. Place a small leaf, centered, on a large leaf and slipstitch it in place. Repeat with the remaining small and large leaves. Slipstitch a pair of combined leaves on either side of the center stem, just below the base of the curved stems. Repeat on the remaining quilt blocks.

6. Quilt Top: Arrange the quilt blocks on a clean, flat surface, in two rows of two, with the stems all pointing toward the lower right-hand corner (see photo). Stitch a 1½ x 23-inch white fabric strip to the bottom edge of the top right square. Stitch the bottom right square to the opposite long edge of the strip. Repeat with the top left and bottom left squares and a second 1½ x 23-inch white fabric strip. Trim the ends of the strips flush with the edges of the quilt blocks. Stitch a 1½-inch square to the short end of a third 1½ x 23-inch white fabric strip, and stitch the remaining strip to the opposite edge of the square. Stitch the combined strip to the right long edge of the first double quilt block. Stitch the second double quilt block to the opposite edge of the combined strip along the quilt block's left edge. Trim the ends of the combined strip flush with the top and bottom edges of the quilt block assembly.

7. Borders: Stitch a 46-inch white border to either side edge of the quilt block assembly, and trim the border ends flush with the top and bottom edges of the assembly. Stitch a 48-inch white border to the top and bottom edges of the assembly, trimming the borders ends flush with the outer edges of the side borders. Stitch the 48- and 50-inch green borders to the white borders of the quilt block assembly in the same way to complete the quilt top.

8. Assembly: Stitch together the green calico quilt back pieces along a long edge to make a quilt back about 60 inches square; press the seam to one side. Place the quilt back, wrong side up, on a clean, flat surface, and tape down the corners. Place the batting, centered, on top of the quilt back. Place the quilt top, centered and right side up, on top of the batting. Starting at the center, working straight out to each edge and diagonally out to each corner, baste through all three layers using long stitches. Add more rows of basting about 4 inches apart, working both vertical and horizontal rows. Remove the tape.

9. Quilting: Place the quilt in a quilting hoop or frame. Use a single quilting thread in the needle. Knot the end of the thread, insert the needle from the back of the quilt and give the thread a small, sharp tug to pull the knot into the batting. Start quilting from the center and work outward. Using small running stitches through all three layers, quilt about ¼ inch from each patch and appliqué seam, stitching on both sides of the seams.

10. Finishing: When the quilting is completed, remove the quilt from the hoop or frame and place it, right side up, on the clean, flat surface. Trim the batting 1½ inches beyond the edges of quilt top. Trim the quilt back 3 inches beyond the edges of the batting. Fold the quilt back edges 1½ inches toward the batting, and press in place. Fold the quilt back edges over the batting another 1½ inches, and slipstitch the pressed quilt back edge to the green border of the quilt top. Remove the basting threads.

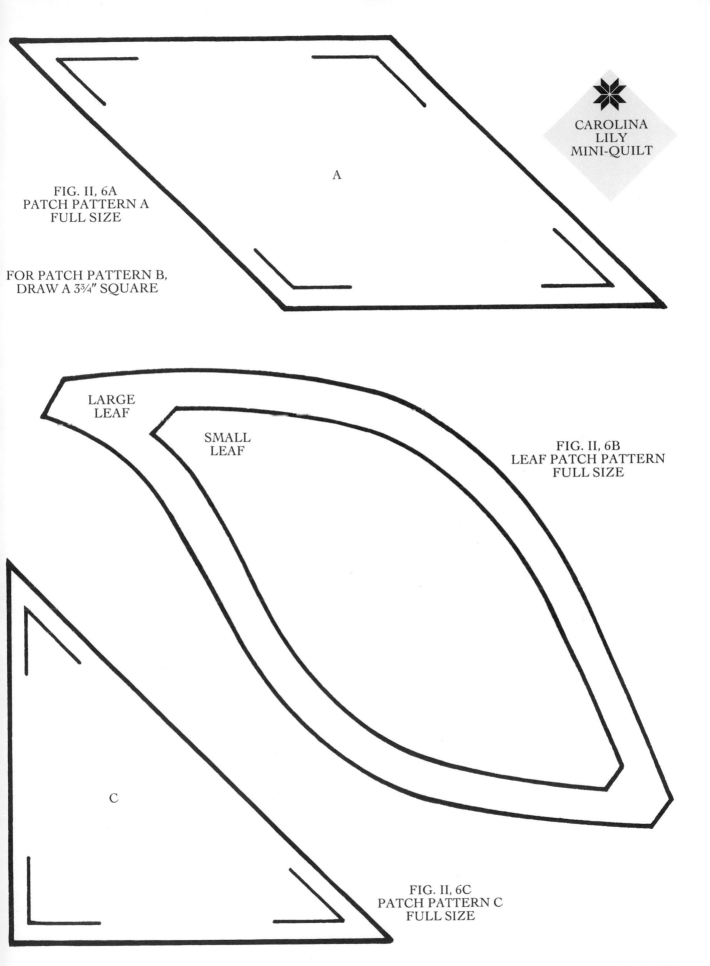

FIG. II, 6A
PATCH PATTERN A
FULL SIZE

FOR PATCH PATTERN B,
DRAW A 3¾″ SQUARE

A

CAROLINA
LILY
MINI-QUILT

LARGE
LEAF

SMALL
LEAF

FIG. II, 6B
LEAF PATCH PATTERN
FULL SIZE

C

FIG. II, 6C
PATCH PATTERN C
FULL SIZE

CRANBERRY STAR MINI-QUILT

CRANBERRY STAR MINI-QUILT

A miniature quilt that combines three favorite patchwork motifs: the eight-point star, the basket and the Flying Geese. Cranberry Star is just the right size for a crib quilt, to top a small table or to use as a wall hanging. Its bright colors and classic motifs will make it a treasured item.

The eight-point star is one of the most popular patchwork motifs. This pattern is pieced from diamond patches, squares, triangles, or some combination thereof. The eight-point star motif is found in antique quilts in many different sizes and used in a variety of ways, and each variation has its own special name. Our "cranberry" star is so named because of the fabrics used, not because of the pattern variation.

The basket motif in each corner of the quilt is known as the "May Basket." There are a seemingly endless list of variations on the motif, including Flower Basket, Fruit Basket, Grape Basket, Grandmother's Basket, Basket of Tulips, Cactus Basket and Garden Basket—just to name a few. Some basket motifs were pieced with patchwork, but many fancier basket designs were appliquéd. These elaborate appliqué baskets were often given curved handles and filled with tiny appliquéd leaves, fruits and flowers made from fabric scraps.

The row of triangular patches used to make the border are known as Flying Geese, Wild Goose or Wild Goose Chase. This is one of the easiest patch patterns to recognize. This patch motif can be used as an overall quilt pattern, with large triangles cut from different fabrics, but because of its simplicity and shape, Flying Geese also was popular for quilt borders.

DIRECTIONS:
(¼-inch seams allowed)

1. Patterns: Draw and cut out all the patterns from the crisp cardboard or manila folder. For the star, draw and cut out two diamonds each with two parallel sides 1½ inches long and the other parallel sides 2⅛ inches long. Label one diamond A; flop the second diamond and label it AR. Draw and cut out a 3-inch square, and a right triangle with two 4¼-inch sides and one 6-inch side. Label the square B and the triangle C. For the May Baskets draw and cut out a right triangle with two 4-inch sides, a right triangle with two 2-inch sides and a 2-inch square. Label the 4-inch triangle D and the 2-inch triangle E. For the handle, draw a half-circle with a 1½-inch circumference and a second half-circle with ⅞-inch circumference centered inside the first; cut out the pattern. For the Flying Geese border, draw and cut out a right triangle with two 2¼-inch sides and one 3-inch side, and a right triangle with two 1½-inch sides and one 2¼-inch side. Label the 2¼-inch triangle F and the 1½-inch triangle G.

2. Cutting: Trace each pattern onto the wrong side of the fabric, and cut out the pieces ¼ inch outside the lines. **From the dark cranberry print,** cut eight A, eight AR and four D. **From the light cranberry print,** cut four A and four AR. **From the medium cranberry print,** cut eight E and 136 G. **From the pindot fabric,** cut four A, four AR, 68 F and four basket handles. **From the off-white fabric,** cut four B, four C, eight D, eight 2-inch squares, and four 6½ x 12½-inch rectangles.

3. Center Star Block: The center star is pieced from eight large diamonds, each of which is made from four A or AR diamonds. Using the photo as a guide, and following Fig. II, 7 (page 56), piece together the eight large diamonds. Begin and end the stitching ¼ inch from the raw edges to allow room for joining; stitch on the drawn lines. With right sides together, stitch a light A below a dark A along a long edge. Stitch a pindot A above a dark A along a long edge. Stitch together the two diamond assemblies, following Fig. II, 7, to complete the large diamond. Repeat with the remaining A patches to make three more large diamonds. Make four AR diamonds in the same way, following Fig. II, 7. Stitch a large A diamond to a large

CHALLENGING:
Requires more experience in quilting.

DIMENSIONS:
About 31" square

MATERIALS:
- 45-inch-wide fabric: ¼ yard each of dark cranberry print, medium cranberry print and light cranberry print; ¼ yard of dark cranberry pindot; 1 yard of dark solid cranberry for quilt back; ½ yard of off-white
- 1 yard of thin synthetic batting
- matching sewing threads
- cranberry quilting thread
- No. 9 quilting needle
- curved needle
- quilting hoop or frame
- crisp cardboard or manila folders
- Basic Quilting Tools, page 137

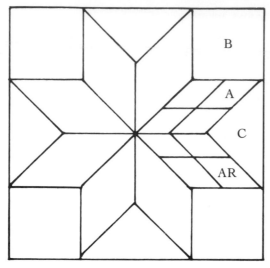

AR diamond along a short edge, with right sides together and light points matching. Repeat to make four pairs of diamonds and stitch the diamonds together alternating A with AR to complete the star. Stitch a B square between the open short edges of the diamonds, and a C triangle between the open long edges, to complete the square (see Fig. II, 7).

4. May Basket: Stitch together a dark D triangle and an off-white D triangle along the long edges. Stitch a short edge of an E triangle to the right-hand side of a 2-inch square, and a second E triangle to the left-hand side of a second 2-inch square. Stitch the triangle/square assemblies to the raw edges of the dark D triangles so the points of the E triangles meet at the corner. Stitch an off-white D triangle to the assembly along the raw edges of the E triangles to complete the block. Using the photo on page 54 as a guide, pin a basket handle to the long dark/off-white seam on the patchwork block. Machine-stitch along both curved edges of the handle, then zigzag stitch over the edges. Turn under the raw ends of the handle and slipstitch them in place (see Stitch Guide, page 146). Repeat to make three more basket squares.

5. Assembly: With right sides together, stitch off-white rectangles, centered, to the top and bottom edges of the star block. Trim the rectangle ends flush with the block. Stitch a basket block to each short edge of the remaining rectangles, placing the baskets so the handles are pointed toward the short ends of the rectangle (see photo). Stitch the basket rectangles to the raw side edges of the star block, with seams matching and basket handles facing the star. Trim the ends flush with the top and bottom edges of the star block.

6. Flying Geese Border: Stitch the long edges of two G triangles to the short edges of an F triangle to form a rectangle. Repeat to make a total of 68 rectangles. With right sides together, stitch a row of 15 rectangles along their long edges with the F triangle points facing the same direction. Repeat to make three more rows of 15 F/G rectangles. Stitch together two of the remaining rectangles along their long pindot edges to make a square. Repeat to make three more squares. Stitch an F/G row to the top and bottom edges of the quilt top with the points facing in opposite directions. Stitch a square to each short end of the remaining F/G rows, then stitch the F/G rows to the sides of the quilt top, matching the seams, so that the points of the F triangles all face the same direction. Press the seams toward the darker fabrics.

7. Basting: Place the quilt back, wrong side up, on a clean, flat surface, and tape down the corners. Place the batting, centered, on top of the quilt back. Place the quilt top, centered and right side up, on top of the batting. Starting at the center, working straight out to each edge and diagonally out to each corner, baste through all three layers using long stitches. Add more rows of basting about 4 inches apart, working both vertical and horizontal rows. Remove the tape.

8. Quilting: Place the quilt in a quilting hoop or frame. Start quilting from the center and work outward. Using small running stitches through all three layers, quilt about ¼ inch from each patch seam, stitching on both sides of the seams. The quilting for the off-white rectangles in the photo was taken from an elaborate stencil pattern. A more simple quilting pattern may be used instead.

9. Finishing: When the quilting is done, trim the batting flush with the quilt top. Trim the quilt back 1 inch beyond the edges of the quilt top. Fold over the raw edges of the quilt back ½ inch, and press. Fold the quilt back over the raw edges of the quilt top, and slipstitch it in place. Remove the basting threads. To hang the quilt, make a casing from extra fabric (see How to Make a Casing, page 145).

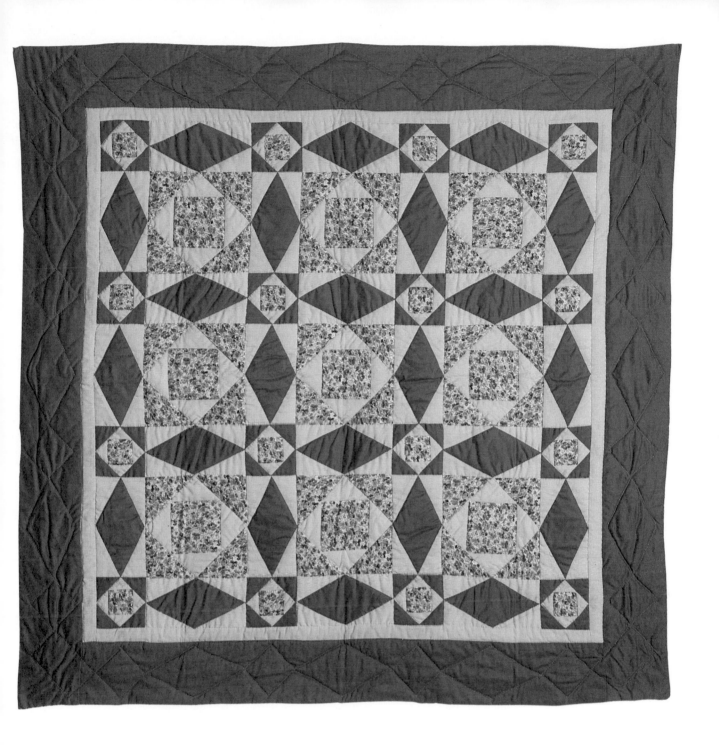

STORM AT SEA QUILT

This beautiful and intricate pattern creates the impression of waves rolling on a rough sea. At first glance, it may appear that the patches are slightly curved, but actually all the patches are perfectly straight-edged diamonds, triangles and squares. The placement of the large and small triangles adjacent to the diamonds creates the illusion of curving "waves."

Storm at Sea is one of the more challenging patchwork patterns in this collection. If you're a beginning quilter, you might want to wait until you've gained some experience before trying your hand with this quilt.

CHALLENGING:
Requires more
experience in quilting.

DIMENSIONS:
Mini-quilt: about 47"
square; double bed:
about 79 x 100"

MATERIALS:

Note: *Quantities for
double bed quilt are given
in parentheses.*

• 45-inch-wide cotton
  fabric:
  1¾ (3) yards of dark
  blue;
  1 (2½) yards of
  medium blue print;
  4¼ (12) yards of solid
  off-white (includes
  quilt back)
• matching sewing
  threads
• matching quilting
  threads
• synthetic batting
• quilting hoop
  or frame
• crisp cardboard
  or manila folders
• dressmaker's pencil
• Basic Quilting Tools,
  page 137

STORM AT SEA QUILT DIRECTIONS:

(¼-inch seams allowed)
Note: Dimensions for double bed quilt are in parentheses.

1. Patterns: Trace the full-size patterns in FIGS. II, 8A-F *(pages 59-61)* onto the crisp cardboard or manila folders. Label the patterns A, B, D, E, F and G as per the diagrams. Also draw a 2¼-inch and a 4-inch square. Label the small square C and the large square H. Cut out the patterns.

2. Cutting: From the dark blue fabric, cut two 5 x 42-inch (5 x 94-inch) side borders, two 5 x 54-inch (5 x 84-inch) top and bottom borders, twenty-four (110) E patches and sixty-four (252) A patches. **From the medium blue print fabric,** cut thirty-six (192) F patches, sixteen (63) C patches and nine (48) H patches. **From the off-white fabric,** cut two 28 x 54-inch (45-inch x 3-yard) quilt back pieces, two 2 x 41-inch (2 x 74-inch) strips, two 2 x 38-inch (2 x 91-inch) strips, sixty-four (252) B patches, ninety-six (440) D patches and thirty-six (192) G patches.

3. Quilt Blocks: When stitching together the patches, begin and end the stitching ¼ inch from the raw edges to allow room for joining. Stitch a B triangle along the long edge to two opposite sides of a C square, then to the top and bottom edge of the square *(see FIG. II, 8G)*. Stitch the long edge of an A triangle to two consecutive B triangle edges. Repeat with three more A triangles to complete the small block. Repeat to make a total of 16 (63) small square blocks. In the same way, using the F, G and H patches, make a total of 9 (48) square quilt blocks *(see FIG. II, 8I, page 61)*. Stitch the long edge of a D triangle to an edge of an E diamond. Repeat with three more D triangles to complete a rectangular quilt block *(see FIG. II, 8H, page 60)*. Repeat with the remaining D and E patches to make a total of 24 (110) rectangular quilt blocks.

4. Quilt Block Rows: Stitch a small square block to the short edge of a rectangular quilt block. Stitch a second small square block to the opposite short edge of the rectangular quilt block. Continue to stitch small square and rectangular blocks together until the row has four (7) small blocks and three (6) rectangular blocks *(see photo, page 57)*.

Repeat to make a total of four (9) small square/rectangular block rows. Stitch the long edge of a rectangular quilt block to one edge of a large square block. Stitch a second rectangular quilt block to the opposite edge of the large square block. Continue to stitch rectangular and large square blocks together until the row has four (7) rectangular blocks and three (6) large square blocks. Repeat to make a total of three (8) rectangular/large square block rows. Stitch together the quilt block rows along their long edges, beginning and ending with a small/rectangular row, and matching the quilt block seams.

5. Borders: Stitch a 38-inch (91-inch) white strip to one side edge of the quilt block assembly, and trim the ends of the strip flush with the assembly. Repeat on the opposite edge of the assembly. Stitch 41-inch (74-inch) white strips to the top and bottom edges of the quilt block assembly, and trim the strip ends flush with the outer edges of the white side strips. Stitch the dark teal border strips to the white strips in the same way to complete the quilt top.

6. Assembly: If the batting needs to be pieced together, spread the pieces on a clean, flat surface with their edges abutted. Work long cross stitches from one batting piece to the other. Stitch together the white quilt back pieces along a long edge to make a 54-inch square (89 x 108-inch rectangle); press the seam to one side. Place the quilt back, wrong side up, on a clean, flat surface, and tape down the corners. Place the batting, centered, on the quilt back. Place the quilt top, centered and right side up, on the batting. Starting at the center, working straight out to each edge and diagonally out to each corner, baste through all three layers using long stitches. Add more rows of basting about 6 inches apart, working both vertical and horizontal rows. Remove the tape.

7. Quilting: Place the quilt in a quilting hoop or frame. Knot the end of a single quilting thread. Insert the needle from the quilt back and give the thread a small, sharp tug to pull the knot into the batting. Start quilting from the center and work outward. Using small running stitches through all three layers, quilt about ¼ inch from each patch and border seam, stitching on both sides of the seams.

6. Finishing: When the quilting is completed, remove the quilt from the hoop or frame and place it, right side up, on the clean, flat surface. Trim the batting flush with the edges of the quilt top. Trim the quilt back 1 inch beyond the edges of the quilt top. Fold the quilt back edges ½ inch toward the batting, and press in place. Fold the quilt back edges another ½ inch over the edges of the quilt top, and slipstitch the folded quilt back edge to the quilt top (*see Stitch Guide, page 146*).

QUILTING PATTERNS

Just like patchwork patterns, quilting patterns have strange and colorful names. From relatively familiar names, such as fleur-de-lis and interlaced diamonds, there is a leap into the mysterious territory of stitching motifs with names like "Cuddy's Lug." Whatever the name, whatever the pattern, it was the stitching, and not the piecework, that was the measure of a quilter's skill in days gone by. Even now, this is how the finest quilts are appraised.

Very often on antique quilts, a quilting pattern used for the central medallion was an extremely elaborate design such as a bouquet of flowers or an American eagle. It is amazing to count just how many different stitching motifs might be used in a particular quilt. Most have at least three: outline quilting around the pieced motifs, a fancy motif for the plain patches or medallions and a repeating border pattern.

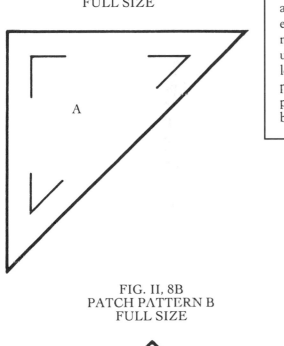

FIG. II, 8A
PATCH PATTERN A
FULL SIZE

FIG. II, 8B
PATCH PATTERN B
FULL SIZE

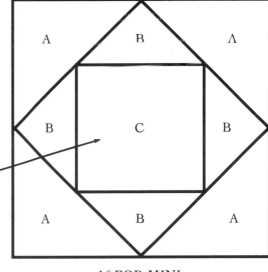

FIG. II, 8G
SMALL SQUARE BLOCK —
4 INCHES FINISHED SIZE

FOR C, CUT
A 2¼″ SQUARE

16 FOR MINI
63 FOR DOUBLE

PATCH	COLOR	MINI	(DBL)
A	DK	64	(252)
B	LT	64	(252)
C	MED	16	(63)

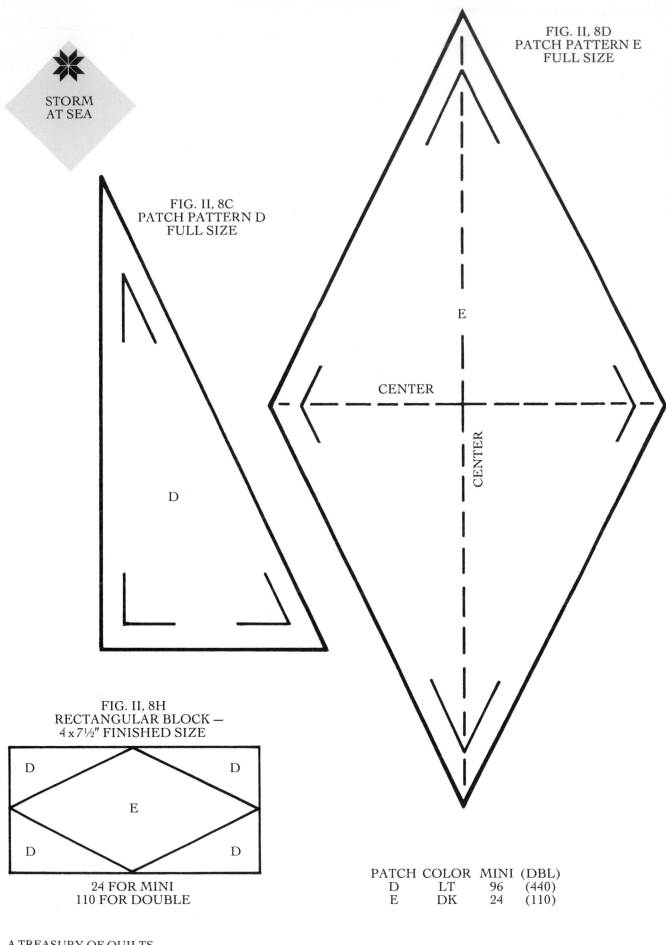

STORM
AT SEA

FIG. II, 8C
PATCH PATTERN D
FULL SIZE

D

FIG. II, 8D
PATCH PATTERN E
FULL SIZE

E

CENTER

CENTER

FIG. II, 8H
RECTANGULAR BLOCK —
4 x 7½" FINISHED SIZE

D   D

E

D   D

24 FOR MINI
110 FOR DOUBLE

PATCH	COLOR	MINI	(DBL)
D	LT	96	(440)
E	DK	24	(110)

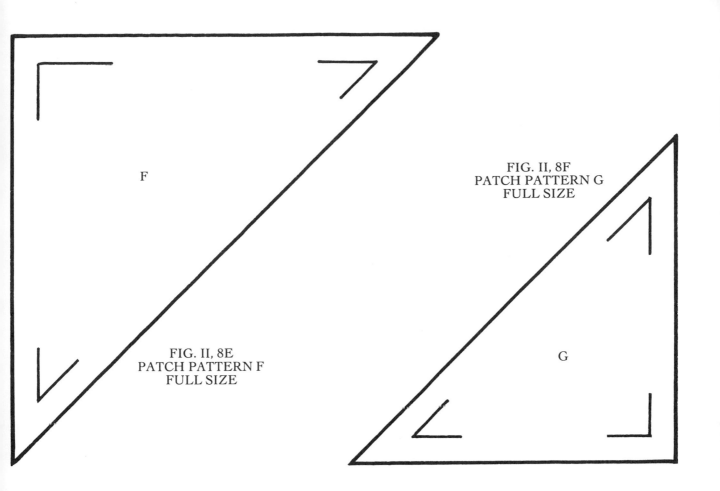

F

FIG. II, 8F
PATCH PATTERN G
FULL SIZE

G

FIG. II, 8E
PATCH PATTERN F
FULL SIZE

PATCH	COLOR	MINI	(DBL)
F	MED	36	(192)
G	LT	36	(192)
H	MED	9	(48)

HANGING QUILTS

Quilts should not be left on a wall for longer than three months at a stretch. To be sure you follow this rule, change your wall hangings with the seasons! When a wall hanging is "off-season," wrap it in acid-free tissue paper, and store it following the directions on page 141.

When hanging a quilt, choose a wall that does not get direct sunlight. The sun can fade the colors of a quilt very quickly.

If the quilt becomes dusty, air it out of doors for a few hours or vacuum it clean (*see Caring for Quilts, page 141*).

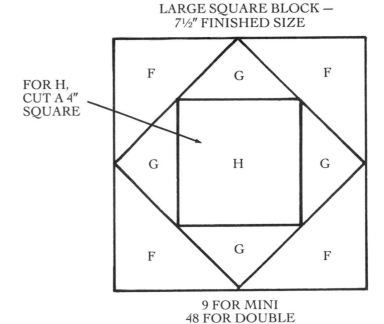

FIG. II, 8I
LARGE SQUARE BLOCK —
7½" FINISHED SIZE

FOR H,
CUT A 4"
SQUARE

F G F

G H G

F G F

9 FOR MINI
48 FOR DOUBLE

SCHOOLHOUSE QUILT

DIMENSIONS:
About 52″ square

MATERIALS:

- 45-inch-wide cotton fabric:
  ¾ yard each of beige print and tan solid;
  ½ yard each of blue pindot and blue print;
  ½ yard of brown pindot;
  4 yards of blue solid (includes quilt back)
- matching sewing threads
- matching quilting threads
- 56-inch square of synthetic batting
- quilting hoop or frame
- crisp cardboard or manila folders
- tracing paper
- dressmaker's pencil
- Basic Quilting Tools, page 137

This rustic quilt with its stencil-like motif celebrates life in rural America. The Schoolhouse Quilt pattern is believed to have originated in New Jersey in the 1870's, when one-room schoolhouses were the norm, and has been a popular design ever since.

Although most Schoolhouse quilts are pieced together, ours is made by appliquéing the parts of the building to large quilt blocks. The Schoolhouse pattern has had many variations over the years. A very innovative quilt might include a different building for each square.

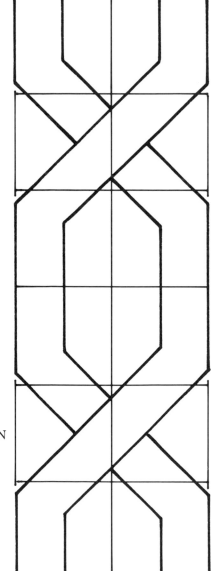

FIG. II, 9A
QUILTING PATTERN
FULL SIZE

DIRECTIONS:
(¼-inch seams allowed)

1. Patterns: Trace the four full-size schoolhouse pattern pieces in FIG. II, 9B *(pages 64-65)* onto the crisp cardboard or manila folders, and cut out the pattern pieces. Trace the full-size chain quilting design in FIG. II, 9A onto the tracing paper, and set aside the quilting pattern.

2. Cutting: From the blue pindot fabric, cut out five sets of schoolhouse patterns. **From the blue print fabric,** cut out four sets of schoolhouse patterns. **From the beige print fabric,** cut five 12½-inch square quilt blocks. **From the tan fabric,** cut four 12½-inch square quilt blocks. **From the brown pindot fabric,** cut two 2 x 42- and two 2 x 45-inch strips, and twenty-four 2-inch squares. **From the blue solid fabric,** cut two 29 x 56-inch quilt back pieces, two 5 x 45-inch and two 5 x 51½-inch borders, and twelve 2 x 12½-inch strips.

3. Quilt Block: On each schoolhouse piece, carefully clip the inner corners of the doors and windows ¼ inch. Turn under the inside edges of the doors and windows ¼ inch, and press in place. Turn under the outside edges of the schoolhouse pieces ¼ inch, and press them in place. Using the photo as a guide, pin a blue pindot schoolhouse to each beige print square, and a blue print schoolhouse to each tan square. Place the pieces 1 inch apart, and center them 1½ inches from the bottom and side edges of the square. Slipstitch the schoolhouse pieces in place *(see Stitch Guide, page 146)*.

4. Quilt Top: Stitch a 2 x 12½-inch blue strip to each side edge of a tan quilt block. Stitch beige print quilt blocks to the long, raw edges of the blue strips to complete the quilt block row *(see photo)*. Repeat to make a second row identical to the first. Stitch blue strips to the side edges of a beige print quilt block, and stitch the remaining tan quilt blocks to the blue strips to complete the center quilt block row. Stitch 2 x 12-inch strips to opposite sides of a brown pindot square. Repeat to make a row of three strips and two squares. Repeat to make a second row of strips and squares. Matching the seams, stitch a blue/brown strip to the bottom edge of the first quilt

(Continued on page 65)

SCHOOLHOUSE QUILT

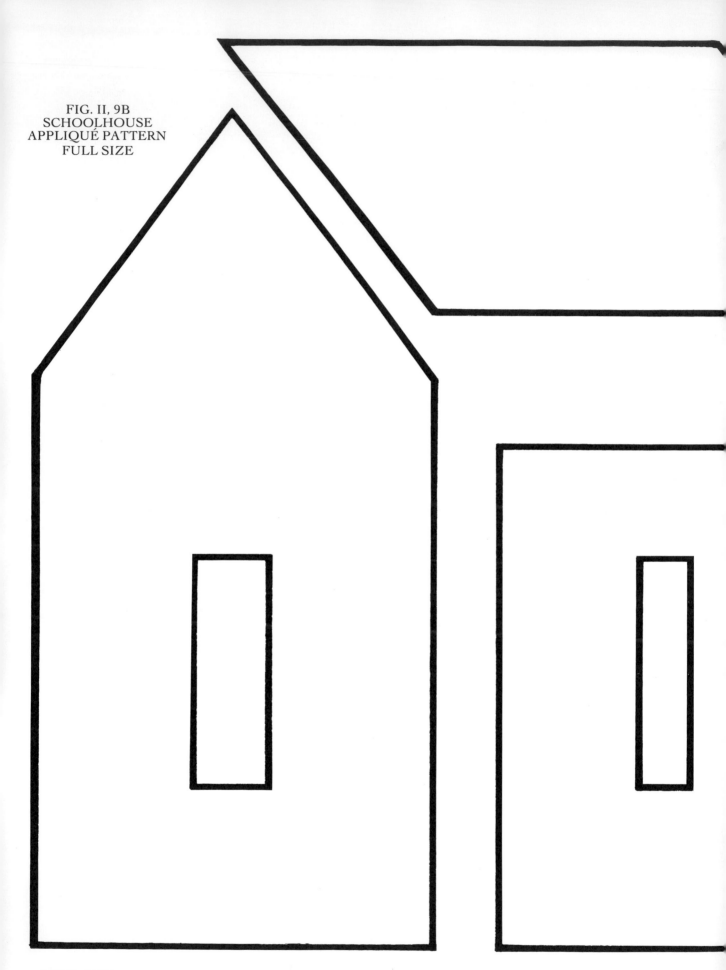

FIG. II, 9B
SCHOOLHOUSE
APPLIQUÉ PATTERN
FULL SIZE

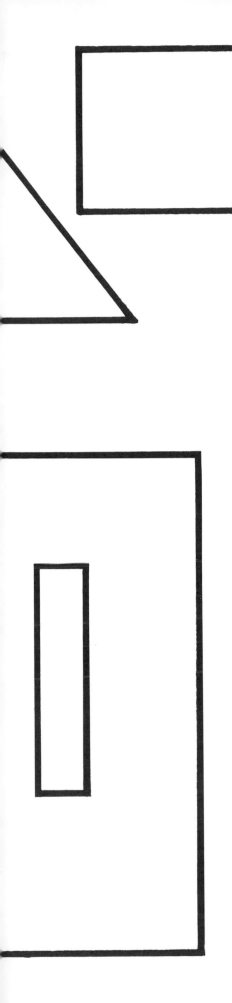

block row (beige/tan/beige) and stitch the second quilt block row (tan/beige/tan) to the bottom edge of the strip. Repeat to attach the remaining strip and quilt block row. Stitch a 2 x 42-inch brown strip to each side edge of the quilt block assembly, and trim the ends flush with the edges of the assembly. Stitch a 2 x 45-inch brown strip to the top and bottom edges of the assembly, and trim the edges flush with the outer edges of the brown side strips.

5. Borders: Stitch a 5 x 45-inch blue border to each side edge of the assembly, trimming the border ends flush with the assembly. Stitch a 5 x 51½-inch blue border to the top and bottom edges of the assembly, trimming the border ends flush with the outer edges of the blue side borders. Using the photo on page 63 as a guide, slipstitch five brown pindot squares to each corner to make a checkerboard, turning under the edges of the squares ¼ inch (*see Stitch Guide*). Using the tracing paper pattern, center and trace the chain quilting design onto the blue border strips.

6. Assembly: Stitch together the quilt back pieces along a long edge to make a 56-inch square, and press the seam to one side. Place the quilt back, wrong side up, on a clean, flat surface, and tape down the corners. Place the batting on top of the quilt back. Place the quilt top, centered and right side up, on top of the batting. Starting at the center, working straight out to each edge and diagonally to each corner, baste through all three layers using long stitches. Add more rows of basting about 4 inches apart, working both vertical and horizontal rows. Remove the tape.

7. Quilting: Place the quilt in a quilting hoop or frame. Start quilting from the center and work outward. Using small running stitches through all three layers, quilt ¼ inch on both sides of all the seams, and over the border chain design.

8. Finishing: Place the quilt, right side up, on the clean, flat surface. Trim the batting flush with the quilt top. Trim the quilt back to ½ inch beyond the quilt top edges. Fold over the raw quilt back edges ¼ inch and press in place. Fold the quilt back edge over the raw edges of the quilt top ¼ inch more, and slipstitch the quilt back edge in place. Remove the basting threads.

SCHOOLHOUSE
QUILT

CARPENTER'S WHEEL MINI-QUILT

DIMENSIONS:
About 45″ square

MATERIALS:
- 45-inch-wide cotton
  broadcloth:
  1¼ yards of gold;
  1¾ yards of green;
  2¾ yards of red
  (includes quilt back)
- matching sewing
  threads
- matching quilting
  threads
- synthetic batting
- quilting hoop
  or frame
- crisp cardboard
  or manila folders
- tracing paper
- dressmaker's pencil
- dressmaker's carbon
  paper (optional)
- Basic Quilting Tools,
  page 137

The eight-point star motif in the center of this quilt is known as the LeMoyne Star—named for Jean Baptiste LeMoyne, who settled Louisiana in 1699 and founded the city of New Orleans in 1718. LeMoyne was not very popular with New Englanders, mostly because he claimed territories in the name of France that the English colonists assumed were their own.

With the Louisiana Purchase in 1803 all was forgiven, and northerners began to appreciate the quilting artistry of the south, including the LeMoyne Star patchwork pattern. The Yankees referred to the pattern as the "Lemon Star"— their own pronunciation of a "foreign" name.

By creating a circle of diamond patches, and placing the patches at right angles to each other, quilt makers developed this variation on the classic LeMoyne star, the Carpenter's Wheel. The quilt top is finished with a sawtooth border to accent the central patchwork motif. Because the patchwork pattern is simple, the quilting motifs are fairly elaborate to add visual interest. A simpler quilting pattern may be substituted, if you wish.

DIRECTIONS:
(¼-inch seams allowed)

1. Patterns: Trace the full-size patterns in Figs. II, 10A and 10B *(pages 68-69)* onto the crisp cardboard or manila folders. Draw a 5½-inch square for pattern C. Cut out and label the patterns. Trace the full-size quilting patterns in Figs. II, 10C and 10D *(page 69)* onto the tracing paper.

2. Cutting: From the green fabric, cut two 5 x 40-inch and two 5 x 50-inch borders, sixteen A diamond patches and four B triangles. Cut fifty 2½-inch squares, then cut the squares in half diagonally to make 100 right triangles. **From the red fabric,** cut two 25 x 48-inch quilt back pieces, eight B triangle patches and sixteen A diamond patches. **From the gold fabric,** cut eight C square patches and twenty B triangle patches. Also cut fifty 2½-inch squares, and cut the squares in half diagonally to make 100 right triangles.

3. Quilt Top: When stitching together the patches, begin and end the stitching ¼ inch from the raw edges to allow room for joining. Stitch a red diamond to a green diamond along one edge. Stitch a red diamond to the opposite edge of the green diamond, and second green diamond to the opposite edge of the second red diamond to make half of the star. Repeat to make a second half star. Press all the seams to one side. Stitch together the two half stars along their long straight edges, and press the center seam open. Pin one edge of a gold square to a star point, right sides together. Starting at the outside point, stitch together the pinned edges, stopping at the seamline. Pivot the assembly, and continue stitching the next square edge to the adjoining star point edge. Repeat until all the star points have gold squares stitched between them. Following Fig. II, 10E *(page 69)*, stitch together the green and red diamonds and triangles, and the gold triangles to complete four corner assemblies. Using the photo as a guide, stitch the four corner assemblies to the center star block.

4. Sawtooth Border: Stitch a 2½-inch gold triangle to a 2½-inch green triangle along their long edges. Repeat to make 100 gold/green squares. Stitch the squares together with the gold triangles facing the same direction, to make four strips of

(Continued on page 68)

CARPENTER'S WHEEL MINI-QUILT

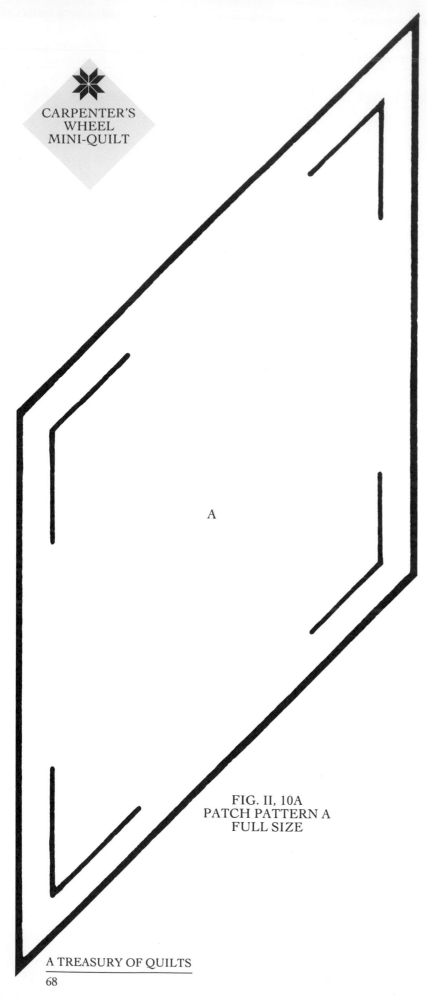

CARPENTER'S WHEEL MINI-QUILT

A

FIG. II, 10A
PATCH PATTERN A
FULL SIZE

25 squares each. Stitch one strip to the edge of the quilt top, green raw edges along the quilt top edge. One end of the sawtooth border should be flush with the side edge of the quilt top; the other end should extend one square beyond the edge of the quilt top. Stitch a second sawtooth border to the adjoining edge of the quilt top, stitching the end of the second border to the extending square of the first. Repeat with the remaining sawtooth borders.

5. Green Border: Stitch the shorter green borders to each side edge of the quilt top. Trim the ends flush with the outer edges of the sawtooth borders and press the seams toward the green borders. Stitch the longer green borders to the top and bottom edges; trim and press them in the same way.

6. Assembly: Stitch together the red quilt back pieces along a long edge; press the seam to one side. Place the quilt back, wrong side up, on a clean, flat surface, and tape down the corners. Place the batting on top of the quilt back. Place the quilt top, centered and right side up, on top of the batting. Starting at the center, working straight out to each edge and diagonally out to each corner, baste through all three layers using long stitches. Add more rows of basting about 4 inches apart, working both vertical and horizontal rows. Remove the tape.

7. Quilting: Using the tracing paper patterns and dressmaker's carbon, and the photo on page 67 as a guide, transfer the wreath pattern to the gold squares, and the pieced corner squares. Transfer the scroll pattern to the green borders. Place the quilt in a quilting hoop or frame. Start quilting from the center and work outward. Using small running stitches through all three layers, quilt ¼ inch from the seams of the diamond patches and the unmarked triangle patches. Quilt over all the drawn quilting lines.

8. Finishing: Place the quilt, right side up, on the clean, flat surface. Trim the batting flush with the quilt top. Trim the quilt back to 1 inch beyond the quilt top edges. Fold over the raw quilt back edges ½ inch and press in place. Fold the quilt back edge over the raw edges of the quilt top ½ inch more, and slipstitch the quilt back edge in place (*see Stitch Guide, page 146*). Remove the basting threads.

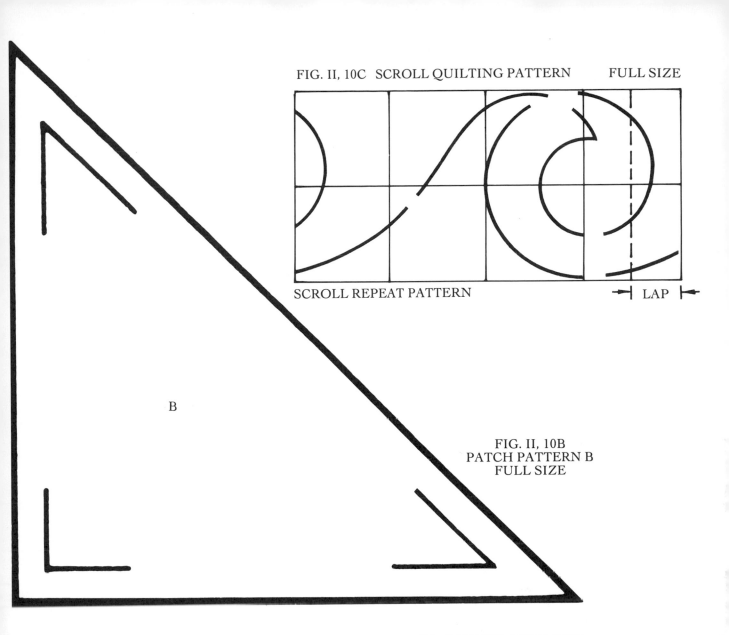

FIG. II, 10C SCROLL QUILTING PATTERN   FULL SIZE

SCROLL REPEAT PATTERN   ←→ LAP ├←

B

FIG. II, 10B
PATCH PATTERN B
FULL SIZE

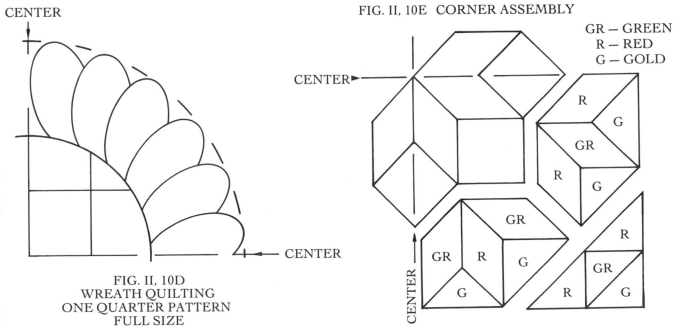

CENTER

CENTER →

FIG. II, 10D
WREATH QUILTING
ONE QUARTER PATTERN
FULL SIZE

FIG. II, 10E CORNER ASSEMBLY

GR — GREEN
R — RED
G — GOLD

CENTER ▶

CENTER

R
G
GR
R
G

GR
GR R G
G
R
GR
R G

QUILTS FOR CHILDREN

FROM A MENAGERIE OF APPLIQUÉD ANIMALS TO BEAUTIFUL PATCHWORK THAT CAN GROW UP WITH YOUR CHILDREN, THE QUILTS IN THIS CHAPTER ARE DESIGNED WITH KIDS IN MIND.

CHILDREN LOVE ANIMALS, SO SEVERAL OF THESE PROJECTS ARE ADORNED WITH WHIMSICAL APPLIQUÉ "CRITTERS." THERE'S A MOTHER HEN WITH HER CHICKS, CALICO DUCKS AND BUNNIES, A KITTY WITH HER FISH, AND A QUILT-FULL OF PINK PIGLETS. THESE QUILTS WILL BRING A SMILE TO ANY CHILD'S FACE.

THERE ALSO ARE MORE TRADITIONAL CRIB QUILTS — SMALLER VERSIONS OF CLASSIC PATCHWORK PATTERNS. THESE BEAUTIFUL QUILTS CAN BE USED FOR A CHILD'S BED NOW, AND LATER USED AS THROWS OR WALL HANGINGS.

EVEN IF YOUR CHILDREN ARE "TOTALLY MODERN," THEY'LL LOVE SNUGGLING UNDER A QUILT MADE JUST FOR THEM. SOME "OLD-FASHIONED" IDEAS NEVER GO OUT OF STYLE.

AMISH SPLIT BARS CRIB QUILT
(directions, page 72)

AMISH SPLIT BARS CRIB QUILT

DIMENSIONS:
About 34 x 42"

MATERIALS:
- 45-inch-wide colorfast cotton: 1½ yards of green (includes quilt back); 1 yard of burgundy; ½ yard of yellow
- 36 x 45-inch piece of synthetic batting
- black or white quilting thread
- dressmaker's pencil
- quilting hoop or frame
- crisp cardboard or manila folders
- tracing paper
- Basic Quilting Tools, page 137

The rich, warm earth tones of this crib quilt provide a unique and welcome change from traditional nursery pastels. The dark shades of green, yellow and burgundy are common colors in Amish quilts—acceptable to the strict rules of the faith. Like most early patchwork, the Amish simply scaled down the size of a quilt to adapt it to a child's bed. The colors of fabric used for full-size coverlets and cribs were the same. As with all Amish quilts, the stitching on this crib quilt is done either in black or white quilt thread.

The patchwork pattern is a classic Split Bars motif which is fairly simple to cut and piece. This motif is often found in full-size quilts. To make a full-size version of the Split Bars quilt, double the length and width measurements of the patches called for in the directions at right.

DIRECTIONS:
(½-inch seams allowed)

1. **Cutting: From the green fabric,** cut a 36 x 45-inch quilt back, three 2 x 31-inch strips, two 3 x 31-inch strips and two 3 x 23-inch strips. **From the burgundy fabric,** cut two 5 x 35-inch borders, two 5 x 27-inch borders and six 2½ x 31-inch strips. **From the yellow fabric,** cut four 3½ x 31-inch strips, four 5-inch squares and four 3-inch squares.

2. **Piecing:** Stitch a 2½ x 31-inch burgundy strip to each long edge of a 2 x 31-inch green strip. Repeat to make a total of three burgundy/green strips. Stitch the yellow strips to the burgundy/green strips along their long edges, alternating the strips, beginning and ending with yellow *(see photo, page 71)*. Stitch the 3 x 31-inch green strips to the raw outer edges of the yellow strips. Stitch 3-inch yellow squares to the short ends of the 3 x 23-inch green strips, then stitch the pieced strips to the top and bottom edges of the striped section, matching the yellow squares to the short ends of the green side edge strips. Press all the seams to one side.

3. **Borders:** Stitch a 5 x 35-inch burgundy border to each long side edge of the quilt top. Stitch a 5-inch yellow square to each short end of the 5 x 27-inch burgundy borders, and stitch one pieced border to the top and bottom edges of the quilt top and the burgundy side borders.

✦ ABOUT CRIB QUILTS

The earliest crib quilts were simply scaled-down versions of the larger quilts made for adult beds. Except for the difference in size, there was little to distinguish a crib quilt from any other quilted or patchwork bed covering.

Some historians believe the reason for this lack of differentiation stems from the sad facts of life in the 17th and 18th centuries. In the days before modern medicine, women bore a great number of children, many of whom would not survive infancy. Crib quilts were deliberately utilitarian, without any sort of personality or individualism, so a quilt could be used for any child; if a baby died, the quilt would not remind the mother of her loss.

As time passed and medical care improved, a child's life expectancy increased and the celebration of children increased accordingly. Children's quilts of the 19th century often were made specifically for a particular child and elaborately decorated with colorful and light-hearted motifs. A popular subject for children's quilts were patriotic motifs—perhaps to inspire loyalty and nationalism in the child who owned the quilt.

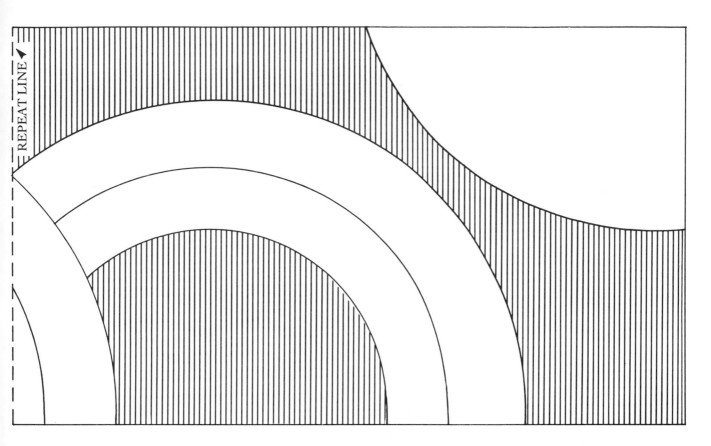

FIG. III, 1
BORDER QUILTING
PATTERN
FULL SIZE

4. Basting: Spread the quilt top, wrong side up, on a clean, flat surface. Place the batting, centered, on top of the quilt top. Starting at the center, working straight out to each edge and diagonally out to each corner, baste through both layers using long stitches. Trim the batting flush with the edges of the quilt top. Spread the quilt back, right side up, on the clean, flat surface. Place the quilt top, batting side up, on top of the quilt back. Pin-baste through all three layers from the center outward, then trim the quilt back flush with the quilt top. Stitch together the quilt layers around three sides and four corners, stitching ½ inch from the raw edges and leaving about 10 inches open along one edge for turning. Trim the batting in the seam allowances close to the stitching. Clip the corners, remove the pins and turn the quilt right side out. Turn in the open edges and slipstitch the opening closed (*see Stitch Guide, page 146*). Pin-baste through all three layers again.

5. Quilting: With a yardstick and the dressmaker's pencil, beginning at the small yellow square in the upper left corner of the quilt top (*not* the border), mark points across the quilt top 2½ inches apart. Repeat on the other three sides of the pieced quilt top; do not draw lines in the burgundy borders or large yellow corner squares. Use the yardstick to connect the points diagonally, in both directions, to form a grid. Place the quilt in a quilting hoop or frame. Start quilting at the center and work outward. Quilt, using a small running stitch through all three layers, over all the marked quilting lines.

6. Border Quilting: Trace the border quilting pattern in Fig. III, 1 onto the crisp cardboard or manila folders. Cut out the white parts of the patterns, but do not cut through the solid lines within each white piece. Save the larger shaded portion for the corner placement. Cut thin slits along the solid lines within the large scallop to trace through. Using a sharp dressmaker's pencil, trace the scallops onto the burgundy borders starting at a corner with a full scallop. Use the shaded pattern to position the scallops at the yellow corner squares. Quilt along the marked quilting lines, as for Step 5.

QUILTS FOR CHILDREN

MOTHER HEN & HER CHICKS

AVERAGE:
For those with some experience in quilting.

DIMENSIONS:
About 44 x 49"

MATERIALS:
- 45-inch-wide fabric:
  1 yard of red print;
  2¼ yards of blue print
  (includes quilt back);
  1 yard of yellow print;
  ½ yard of white print
- matching quilting thread
- red and blue sewing threads
- 45 x 60-inches of synthetic batting
- crisp cardboard or manila folders
- dressmaker's pencil
- Basic Quilting Tools, page 137

Here's a farm-fresh family appliquéd in country colors. The mother hen is leading her chicks in the right direction, but there's always one who won't run with the pack!

This quilt also makes a wonderful wall hanging for a child's room (or a kitchen!). Just omit the red print borders and add a casing to the quilt back (see How to Make a Casing, page 145).

❋ ANIMAL QUILTS

Children are forever drawn to, and fascinated by, animals. Whether it's the family dog or a horse grazing in a field, animals inspire a child's natural affection and instantly command her attention.

Traditionally, quilts were decorated with motifs that were significant to their owners, so it seems fitting that many children's quilts of years gone by feature animal motifs. Animals appear on quilts in a variety of forms. During the Victorian era, Crazy Quilts often featured many creatures, beautifully embroidered, including birds, spiders and spider webs, even children themselves.

DIRECTIONS:
(½-inch seams allowed)

1. Patterns: Trace the appliqué pattern pieces in Figs. III, 2A-2F *(pages 76-79)* onto crisp cardboard or manila folders, and cut out the patterns. Enlarge the mother hen pattern in Fig. III, 2G *(pages 80-81)* onto cardboard, following the directions on page 145, and cut out the pattern.

2. Cutting: When cutting out the appliqué fabric pieces, cut ¼ inch beyond the drawn lines. **From blue fabric,** cut a 26 x 31-inch quilt top and a 45 x 50-inch quilt back. **From yellow fabric,** cut two 5 x 31-inch borders, two 5 x 26-inch borders, one wing, one foot, one beak, five chicks (flop the pattern for one chick). **From red fabric,** cut two 6½ x 39-inch borders, two 6½ x 45-inch borders, four hearts and one scarf. **From white fabric,** cut four 5-inch squares and one hen body.

3. Appliqués: Pin one red heart, centered, to each white square. Using red sewing thread, stitch over the drawn lines. Trim the red fabric close to the stitching. Using a wide, close machine zigzag stitch, stitch around the edges of the heart. Using the photo as a guide, pin the mother hen, foot and beak to the quilt top, overlapping as necessary. Using blue sewing thread, stitch and machine appliqué the hen pieces to the quilt top in the same way as for the hearts. Pin the wing and scarf to the hen, and machine appliqué as above. Repeat for the chicks, overlapping as necessary. Zigzag stitch around the eyes of the hen and chicks, and straight stitch over the broken lines of the wings and scarf.

4. Quilt Top: Stitch a 5 x 31-inch yellow border to each side edge of the quilt top. Stitch an appliquéd white square to each short end of the remaining yellow borders, then stitch the borders to the top and bottom edges of the quilt top. Stitch a 6½ x 39-inch red border to each side edge, then stitch 6½ x 45-inch red borders to the top and bottom edges of the quilt top.

5. Assembly: Spread the quilt top, wrong side up, on a clean, flat surface and tape down the corners. Place the batting, centered, on the quilt top and pin through both layers. Starting at the center of the quilt, baste outward through both layers with long stitches, straight to each edge and diagonally to each corner. Add more

(Continued on page 77)

MOTHER HEN & HER CHICKS

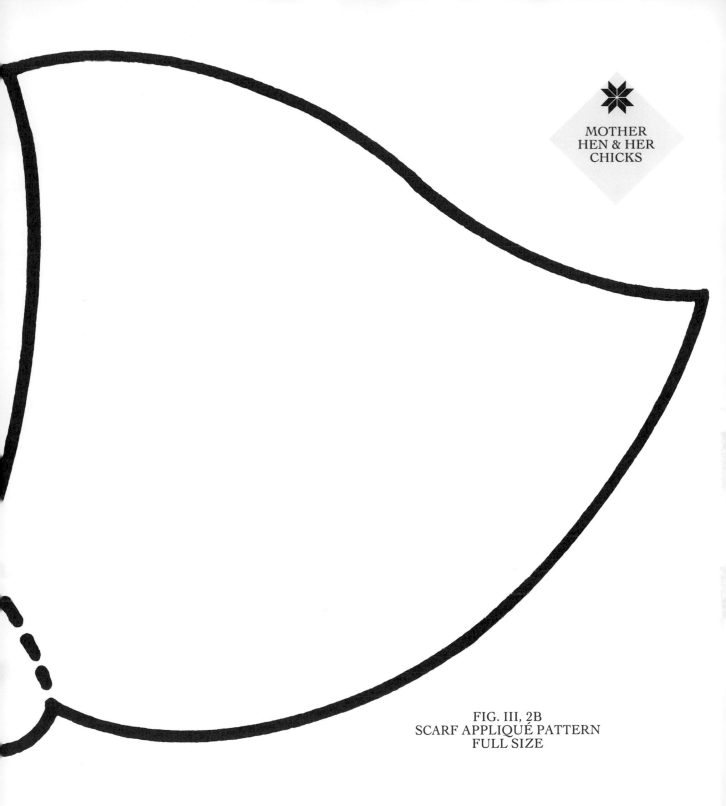

FIG. III, 2B
SCARF APPLIQUÉ PATTERN
FULL SIZE

vertical and horizontal rows of basting about 6 inches apart. Trim the batting flush with the quilt top. Remove the tape. Pin the quilt top to the quilt back, right sides together and raw edges matching. Stitch together the quilt layers around three sides and four corners, leaving a 15-inch opening on one side for turning. Remove the pins. Turn the quilt right side out, and slipstitch the opening closed (*see Stitch Guide, page 146*). Quilt, using small running stitches through all three layers, over all the border seams. Remove the basting threads.

FIG. III, 2C
WING APPLIQUÉ PATTERN
FULL SIZE

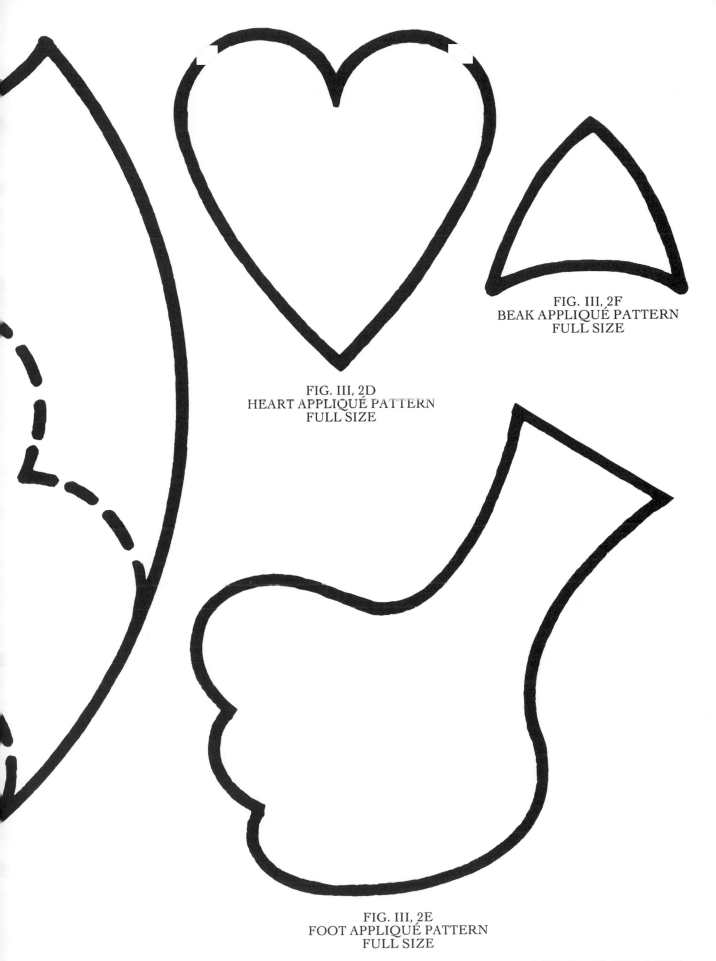

FIG. III, 2F
BEAK APPLIQUÉ PATTERN
FULL SIZE

FIG. III, 2D
HEART APPLIQUÉ PATTERN
FULL SIZE

FIG. III, 2E
FOOT APPLIQUÉ PATTERN
FULL SIZE

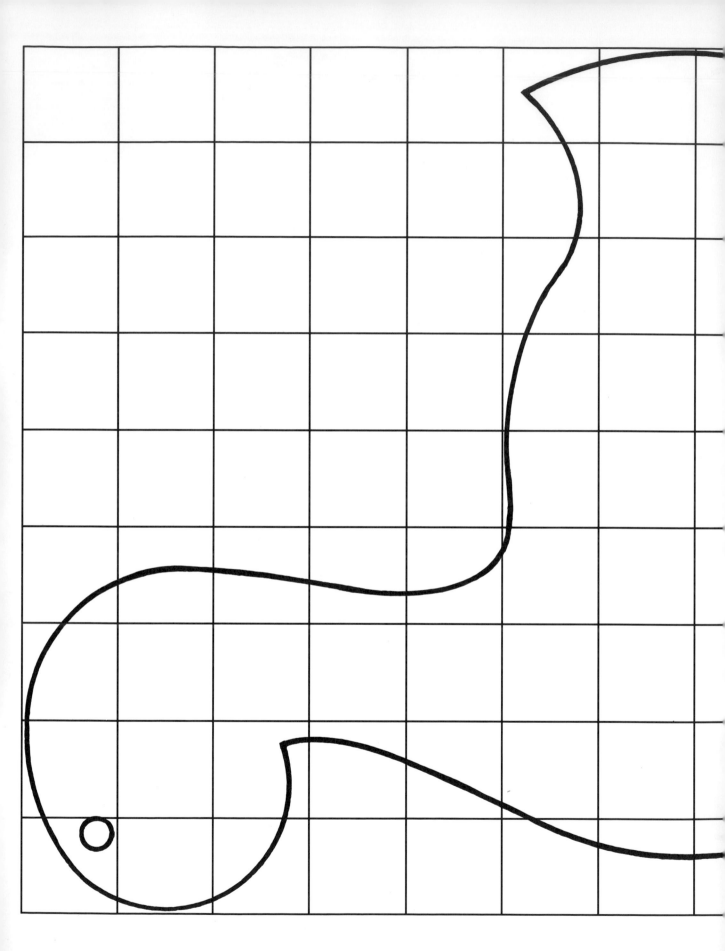

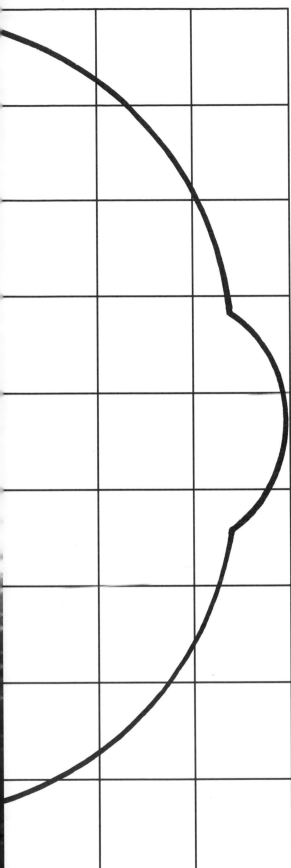

LITTLE CHICK PILLOW

DIRECTIONS:
(½-inch seams allowed)

1. Pattern: Trace the full-size chick appliqué pattern in Fɪɢ. III, 2A *(page 76)* onto crisp cardboard or a manila folder, and cut out the pattern.

2. Cutting: From the yellow fabric, cut two 2½ x 10-inch borders, two 2½ x 13-inch borders, one 2¾ x 130-inch ruffle strip, pieced as needed, and one chick. **From the red fabric,** cut a 5 x 130-inch ruffle strip, pieced as needed, and a 13-inch square pillow back.

3. Appliqué: Stitch the chick, centered, to the blue square following Step 3 of Mother Hen & Her Chicks Quilt *(page 74)*. Stitch a 2½ x 10-inch yellow border to either side edge of the appliquéd square, then stitch the 2½ x 13-inch borders to the top and bottom edges of the square.

4. Ruffles: Stitch together the short ends of each ruffle strip to make a loop. Stitch a ¼-inch hem along one long edge of each loop. Stitch two gathering rows ¼-inch and ½-inch from the opposite raw edge. Pull up the gathers until each loop measures 53 inches. Pin the yellow ruffle on top of the red one, raw edges even, and stitch the ruffles together over the gathering stitches. Pin the double ruffle to the pillow top, right sides together and raw edges matching, and stitch in place.

5. Assembly: Pin the pillow back to the pillow top, right sides together, raw edges matching and the ruffles inside toward the center. Stitch together the pillow back and the pillow top around three sides and four corners, leaving an opening on one side for turning. Turn the pillow right side out and stuff it firmly. Turn in the open edges and slipstitch the opening closed *(see Stitch Guide, page 146)*.

AVERAGE:
For those with some experience in quilting.

DIMENSIONS:
About 12″ square, plus ruffle

MATERIALS:
- 10-inch square of blue print fabric
- 45-inch-wide fabric: ½ yard of yellow print; ¾ yard of red print (includes pillow back)
- blue sewing thread
- synthetic stuffing
- crisp cardboard or manila folders
- dressmaker's pencil
- Basic Quilting Tools, page 137

**FIG. III, 2G
MOTHER HEN APPLIQUÉ PATTERN
1 SQ. = 2″**

 AN APPLIQUÉ CLIP TIP

Use small, sharp embroidery scissors to clip curved seams and the edges of appliqué patches. This helps to smooth the curved edges so they will lie flat as you stitch the appliqué in place.

CALICO DUCKS N' BUNNIES SET

This crib set combines a variety of colorful fabrics in an enchanting design. First strips of fabric are pieced together to make the quilt or pillow top, then the ducks, bunnies, carrots and tulips are appliquéd on top of the fabric strips. Piecing together ten different prints and solid fabrics make this set a challenge for any quilter.

We suggest making the pillow before attempting the quilt in order to practice the combination of patchwork and appliqué techniques used to make these projects. Although the techniques themselves may be familiar, this particular pattern is quite intricate and can be tricky to stitch together.

CHALLENGING:
Requires more experience in quilting.

DIMENSIONS:
About 37 x 45″

MATERIALS:
- 45-inch-wide cotton: 1¾ yards of blue and white stripe (E); ⅓ yard each of dark green solid (C), dark blue solid (D), dark green calico (F), dark blue calico (H) and light blue calico (J); ¼ yard each of white and rust calico (A), rust calico (B) and blue floral print (G); ⅛ yard of green and white stripe (I)
- matching sewing threads
- matching quilting threads
- 45 x 60-inch piece of synthetic batting
- crisp cardboard or manila folders
- glue stick
- tracing paper
- fabric marking pen
- Basic Quilting Tools, page 137

BUNNY QUILT DIRECTIONS:
(¼-inch seams allowed)

1. Patterns: The appliqué patterns are designed for machine appliqué; if appliquéing by hand, add a ¼-inch seam allowance around each appliqué pattern (not the triangle template). Trace the full-size appliqué patterns and the triangle template in FIGS. III, 3A-3F (*pages 84-85*) onto tracing paper. Make separate patterns for the carrot top and the bunny's bow. Glue the tracing paper patterns to the crisp cardboard or manila folders, and cut out the patterns and template.

2. Cutting: From A, cut 5 small bunnies facing left, 1 large bunny facing left, 4 hearts, and 8 triangles. **From B,** cut 4 small bunnies facing right, 3 large bunnies facing right, 2 large bunnies facing left, and 10 carrots. **From C,** cut 10 carrot tops, 8 tulips, 8 triangles, and one 2 x 44-inch strip. **From D,** cut 3 bows facing right, 3 bows facing left, 8 triangles, one 4½ x 44-inch strip, and one 2 x 44-inch strip. **From E,** cut one 4½ x 44-inch strip, and one 39 x 47-inch piece for quilt back. **From F,** cut one 4½ x 44-inch strip, one 2 x 44-inch strip, and 8 triangles. **From G,** cut 8 triangles, and two 2 x 44-inch strips. **From H,** cut 8 triangles, one 4½ x 44-inch strip, and one 2 x 44-inch strip. **From I,** cut one 2 x 44-inch strip. **From J,** cut five 2 x 44-inch strips.

3. Patchwork Rows: With right sides facing, stitch a C triangle to an F triangle along their long edges to form a square. Repeat with the remaining C and F triangles to make a total of eight squares. With right sides facing, stitch the squares together along their matching short edges to make a row, beginning and ending with a C triangle. Press all seams to one side. Repeat to make a patchwork row of D and H triangles, beginning and ending with D, and a patchwork row of A and G triangles, beginning and ending with A.

4. Quilt Top Assembly: Using the photo as a guide, stitch together the patchwork rows and fabric strips in the following order, pressing the seams to one side.
Row 1: C/F patchwork row, F long edges at the top.
Row 2: 4½ x 44-inch H strip.
Row 3: 2 x 44-inch I strip.
Row 4: 2 x 44-inch F strip.

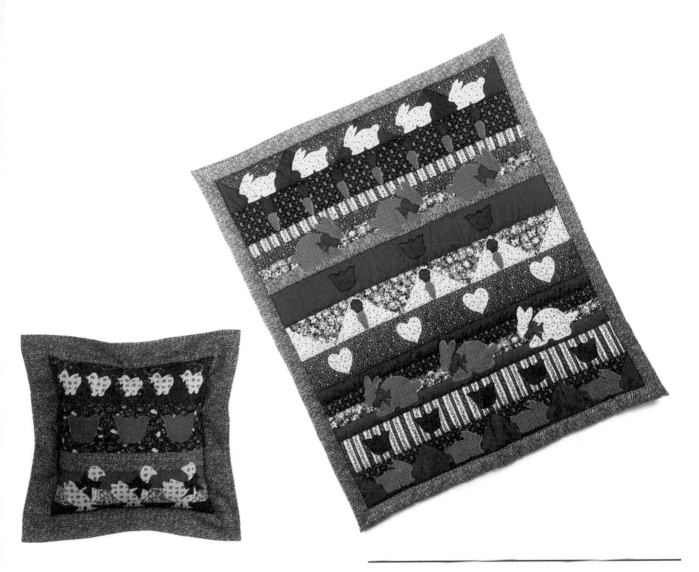

CALICO DUCKS N' BUNNIES SET

Row 5: 2 x 44-inch G strip.
Row 6: 2 x 44-inch J strip.
Row 7: 4½ x 44-inch D strip.
Row 8: A/G patchwork row, G long edges at the top.
Row 9: 4½ x 44-inch F strip.
Row 10: 2 x 44-inch C strip.
Row 11: 2 x 44-inch H strip.
Row 12: 2 x 44-inch G strip.
Row 13: 2 x 44-inch D strip.
Row 14: 4½ x 44-inch E strip.
Row 15: D/H patchwork row, H long edges at the top.
Trim the side edges of the pieced quilt top just until they are even.

5. Appliqué: Using the photo as a guide, pin the appliqué pieces to the quilt top.
Row 1: 5 small A bunnies.
Row 2: 7 carrots and tops, overlapping as shown in Fig. III, 3D.
Rows 3 to 6: 3 large D bunnies and bows, facing right.
Row 7: 3 tulips.
Row 8: 3 carrots and tops (see Row 2).
Row 9: 4 hearts.
Rows 10 to 13: Remaining large bunnies and bows.
Row 14: 5 tulips.
Row 15: 4 small D bunnies. Edgestitch very close to the raw edges around all of

the appliqués. To finish, stitch over all the appliqué edges using a close zigzag stitch.

6. Borders: Press the quilt top on its wrong side. Stitch a 2 x 44-inch J border strip, centered, to each side edge of the quilt top. Repeat with the remaining J border strips for the top and bottom borders. Miter the border ends and stitch them together.

7. Assembly: Spread the batting on a clean, flat surface. Place the quilt back, right side up, on top of the batting, and the quilt top, wrong side up and centered, on top of the quilt back. Starting at the center, working straight out to each edge and diagonally out to each corner, pin-baste through all three layers. Trim the batting and the quilt back flush with the quilt top. Using a loose (6 to 8 stitches per inch) straight stitch, machine-stitch around three sides and four corners, leaving an 8- to 10-inch opening along one edge. Remove the pins. Turn the quilt right side out and slipstitch the opening closed *(see Stitch Guide, page 146).*

8. Quilting: Using small running stitches through all three layers, quilt ¼-inch inside the border seam and on both sides of the row seams of the quilt top. Do not stitch over the appliqués.

(Continued on page 86)

WEAR & TEAR FABRICS

Save fancy fabrics for decorative quilts and wall hangings. Easy-care fabrics are the best choice for quilts that will get a lot of wear.

When making quilts for babies and children, select washable cotton or polyester/cotton fabrics. Be sure the fabrics are colorfast and pre-shrunk. Always wash and iron fabrics before you use them.

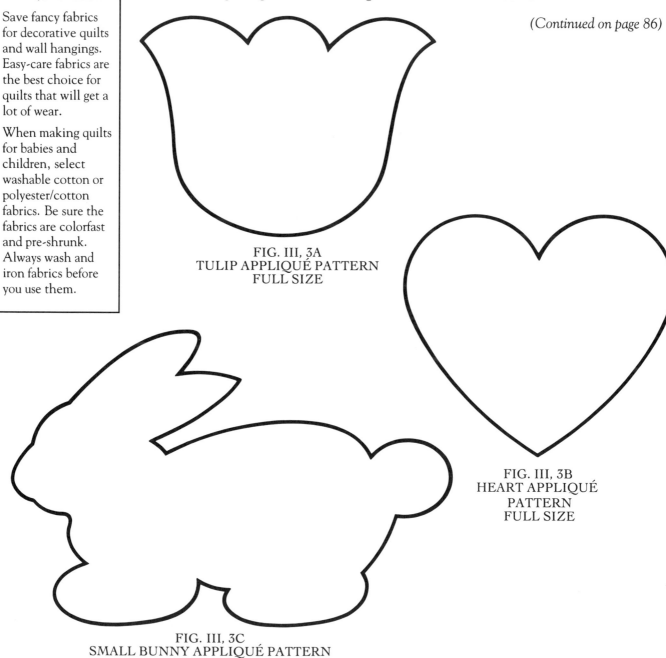

FIG. III, 3A
TULIP APPLIQUÉ PATTERN
FULL SIZE

FIG. III, 3B
HEART APPLIQUÉ
PATTERN
FULL SIZE

FIG. III, 3C
SMALL BUNNY APPLIQUÉ PATTERN
FULL SIZE

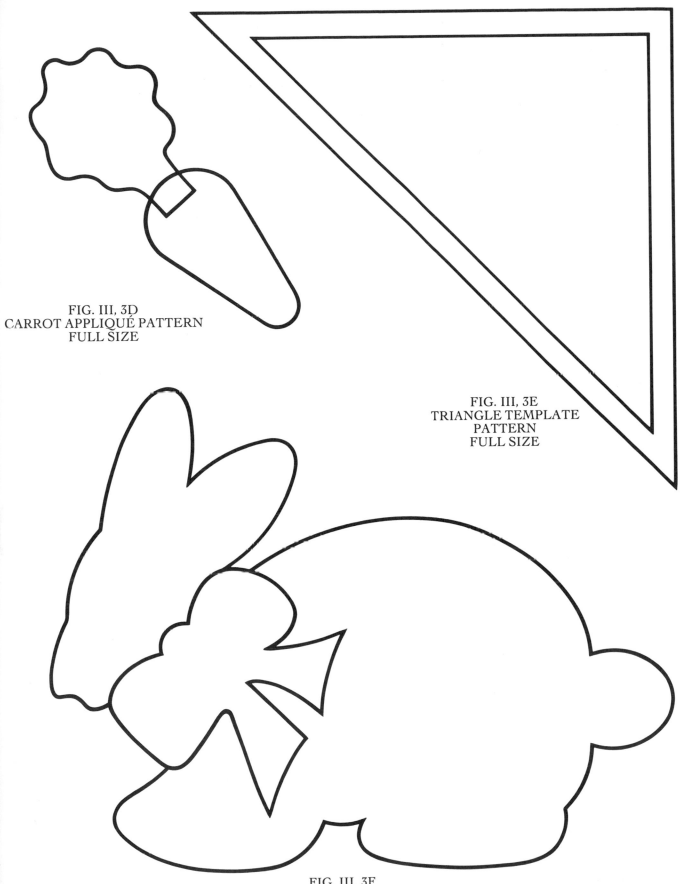

FIG. III, 3D
CARROT APPLIQUÉ PATTERN
FULL SIZE

FIG. III, 3E
TRIANGLE TEMPLATE
PATTERN
FULL SIZE

FIG. III, 3F
LARGE BUNNY APPLIQUÉ PATTERN
FULL SIZE

DUCK PILLOW

DIMENSIONS:
14″ square, plus
2″ borders

MATERIALS:
- 45-inch-wide cotton:
  ⅔ yard of blue
  calico (E);
  ⅓ yard of medium
  blue calico (F);
  ¼ yard of navy blue
  solid (A);
  ⅛ yard each of dark
  green calico (B),
  dark green solid (C),
  medium green calico
  (D) and yellow
  calico (G)
- matching sewing
  threads
- 14-inch-square
  synthetic pillow form
- 12-inch-long
  blue zipper
- crisp cardboard
  or manila folders
- tracing paper
- fabric marking pen
- glue stick
- Basic Quilting Tools,
  page 137

DIRECTIONS:
(¼-inch seams allowed)

1. Patterns: The appliqué patterns are designed for machine appliqué; if appliquéing by hand, add a ¼-inch seam allowance to the appliqué pieces (not the triangle templates). Trace the full-size patterns in FIGS. III, 3G-3L onto tracing paper. Make separate patterns for the ducks' bows. Glue the tracing paper to the crisp cardboard or manila folders, and cut out the patterns.

2. Cutting: From A, cut one each of Template 1 and Template 2, flop the pattern and cut one more of each, one 2 x 15-inch strip, two bows facing right and one bow facing left. **From B,** cut one 2 x 15-inch strip. **From C,** cut 3 tulips and one 2 x 15-inch strip. **From D,** cut Template 1 and Template 2 as for Color A. **From E,** cut one 4½ x 15-inch strip and two 8 x 15-inch rectangles for pillow back. **From F,** cut one 2 x 15-inch strip, two 5 x 15-inch strips and two 5 x 19-inch strips for pillow ruffle. **From G,** cut five ducklings facing left, two ducks facing right and one duck facing left.

3. Piecing: With right sides facing, stitch the A triangles to their corresponding D triangles along their long edges. You will have two squares and two rectangles. To make the patchwork row, stitch together a square, rectangle, rectangle and square, matching the fabrics at each seam, beginning and ending with Color D. Assemble the pillow top in rows as follows:
Row 1: A/D patchwork row.
Row 2: 4½ x 15-inch E strip.
Row 3: 2 x 15-inch F strip.
Row 4: 2 x 15-inch C strip.
Row 5: 2 x 15-inch B strip.
Row 6: 2 x 15-inch A strip.

4. Appliqué: Using the photo on page 83 as a guide, center and pin 5 ducklings on Row 1, 3 tulips on Row 2 and 3 ducks on Rows 3-6, with the left-facing duck on the far right end. Pin the bows to the ducks' necks. Appliqué all the pieces following Step 5 of the Bunny Quilt *(page 83)*.

5. Finishing: Set the zipper, centered, between the two 8 x 15-inch E rectangles, along their long edges. Trim the pillow back flush with the pillow top. Stitch a

5 x 15-inch ruffle strip, right sides facing, to each side edge of the pillow top. Repeat with the 5 x 19-inch strips on the top and bottom edges of the pillow top. Fold the ruffle strips in half, long edges matching, and press along the fold. Pin the ruffles flat against the right side of the pillow top. Pin the pillow back to the pillow top, right sides together, and stitch around all the edges, catching in the raw edge of the ruffle as you stitch. Turn the pillow right side out through the zipper opening and press. Topstitch around the pillow on the ruffle seamline. Insert the pillow form.

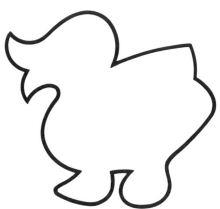

FIG. III, 3G
DUCKLING APPLIQUÉ PATTERN
FULL SIZE

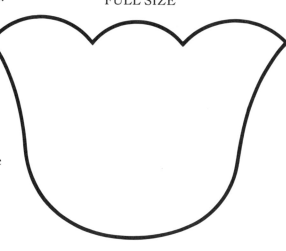

FIG. III, 3H
TULIP APPLIQUÉ PATTERN
FULL SIZE

FIG. III, 3I
TRIANGLE
TEMPLATE 1
PATTERN
FULL SIZE

FIG. III, 3J
RIGHT DUCK APPLIQUÉ PATTERN
FULL SIZE

FIG. III, 3K
LEFT DUCK APPLIQUÉ PATTERN
FULL SIZE

FIG. III, 3L
TRIANGLE TEMPLATE 2 PATTERN
FULL SIZE

CAT & FISH QUILT AND PILLOW SET

■

AVERAGE:
For those with some experience in quilting.

DIMENSIONS:
About 40 x 53"

MATERIALS:
- 45-inch-wide fabric:
  2¼ yards of green check;
  ½ yard of white check;
  1½ yards of small yellow check;
  ¾ yard of yellow print
- 45 x 60-inch piece of synthetic batting
- 2 yards of lightweight fusible interfacing
- 3 spools of green sewing thread
- yellow quilting thread
- crisp cardboard or manila folders
- fabric marking pen
- dressmaker's pencil
- quilting hoop or frame
- Basic Quilting Tools, page 137

A bright, whimsical quilt and pillow set that will delight any child — these stalking cats never catch their fish!

This appliqué block pattern lends itself to many color variations. Choose a child's favorite colors, or make each cat and fish a different color. Because the patchwork is simple, the quilting can be more elaborate. If you wish, embroider realistic details on the appliqué pieces, or add wild and wonderful decorations such as collars and bells on the cats, and sequin "scales" on the fish. If the set is for very small children, do not add anything that might be pulled off by curious little fingers.

A QUILTED GIFT

When giving a quilt as a gift, be sure to include care instructions in the gift box. Quilts must be cleaned and aired carefully to keep their colors and stitching from deteriorating. See page 141 for tips on quilt care.

Another lovely touch: personalize the quilt by embroidering or quilting the recipient's name and the date or the occasion somewhere on the quilt top.

CAT & FISH QUILT DIRECTIONS:
(½-inch seams allowed)

1. Pattern: Trace the full-size cat and fish appliqué patterns in FIGS. III, 4A and 4B *(pages 90-91)* onto the crisp cardboard or manila folders, and cut out the patterns. Cut out the slits along the top of the cat's back leg and under it's chin. Cut out the eyes on the cat and fish.

2. Cutting: From the green check fabric, cut a 44¼ x 59¼-inch quilt back/border and four 11 x 15¾-inch square blocks. **From the white check fabric,** cut four 11 x 15¾-inch square blocks. **From the small yellow check fabric,** cut three 3¼ x 47¾-inch strips, two 3¼ x 37¼-inch strips, six 3¼ x 15¾-inch strips, four fish facing right and four fish facing left. **From the yellow print fabric,** fuse the interfacing to the wrong side of the fabric, then cut out four cats facing right and four cats facing left. Using the dressmaker's pencil, lightly mark the slits over the leg and under the chin on the fabric cats, and outline the eyes on the cats and fish.

3. Appliqués: Using the photo as a guide, pin a cat and a fish to each green check and white check square. Make two of each color with the appliqués facing left and two of each facing right. Using the green thread, satin stitch around all the edges of the appliqués. Stitch over the marked lines to define the cat's hind leg and chin, and the cat and fish eyes.

4. Quilt Top: With right sides together, stitch together a vertical row of right-facing appliqué blocks with 3¼ x 15¾-inch yellow strips between them, beginning and ending with a quilt block. Alternate the block background colors *(see photo)*. Repeat to make a vertical row of left-facing appliqué blocks. Stitch the block rows to either edge of a 3¼ x 47¾-inch yellow strip so all the cats are facing the center strip. Stitch the remaining 47¾-inch strips to the outer raw edges of the block rows. Stitch the 3¼ x 37¼-inch strips to the top and bottom edges of the quilt top.

5. Assembly: Place the quilt back, wrong side up, on a clean, flat surface, and tape down the corners. Place the batting on top of the quilt back, and trim the batting edges flush with the quilt back. Baste through both layers ½ inch from the edges. Trim the batting to the basting

(Continued on page 90)

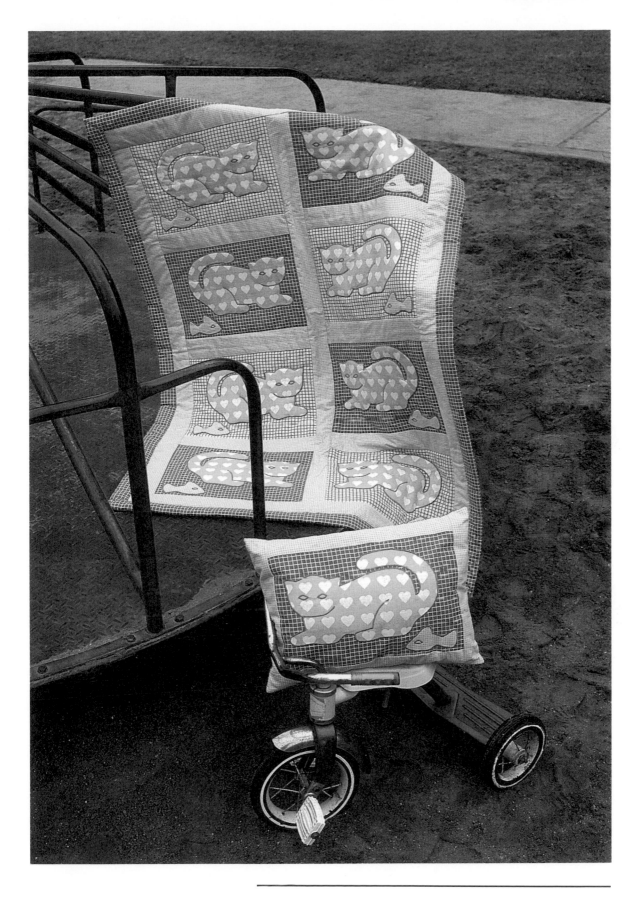

CAT & FISH QUILT AND PILLOW SET

**CAT & FISH
QUILT &
PILLOW SET**

lines. Place the quilt top, centered and right side up, on top of the batting. Starting at the center, working straight out to each edge and diagonally to each corner, baste through all three layers. Add vertical and horizontal rows of basting about 6 inches apart. Remove the tape.

6. Quilting: Place the quilt in a quilting hoop or frame. Start quilting from the center and work outward. Using small running stitches through all three layers, quilt around each cat and fish motif, then over the cat's leg and chin lines. Quilt along each seamline, and remove the basting threads.

7. Border: Fold over the edges of the quilt back ½ inch and press the fold. Bring the folded quilt back edges over the extending batting and pin the edges ½ inch in from the raw edges of the quilt top to form a border. Slipstitch the quilt back/border edge to the quilt top, mitering the corners of the border as you stitch *(see Stitch Guide, page 146)*.

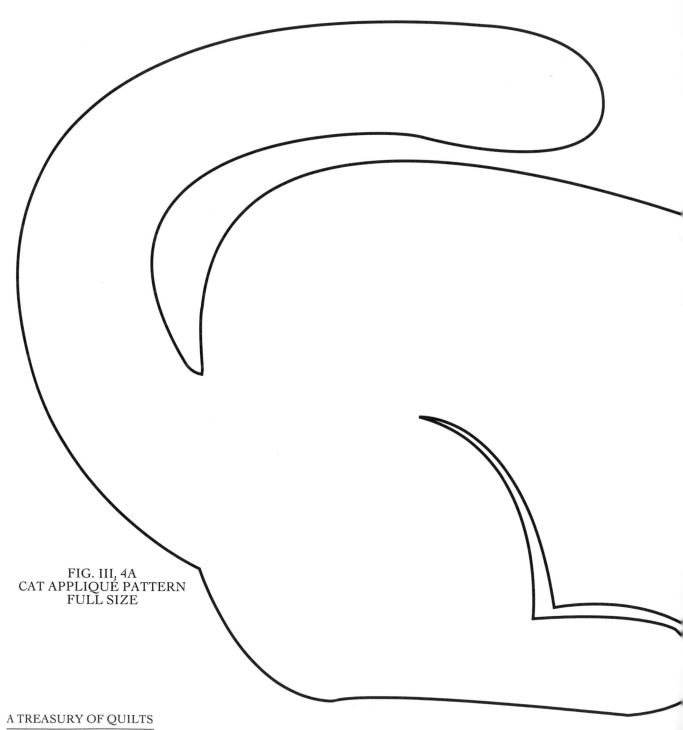

FIG. III, 4A
CAT APPLIQUÉ PATTERN
FULL SIZE

CAT & FISH PILLOW

DIRECTIONS:

1. Pattern: Trace the full-size cat and fish patterns in Figs. III, 4A and 4B onto crisp cardboard or manila folders, and cut out the patterns. Cut out the slits along the top of the cat's back leg and under it's chin. Cut out the eyes on the cat and fish.

2. Cutting: From the green check fabric, cut one 11 x 16-inch pillow top and one 15 x 20-inch pillow back. **From the small yellow check fabric,** cut two 3 x 16-inch borders, two 3 x 15-inch borders and one fish. **From the yellow print fabric,** fuse the interfacing to the wrong side of the fabric and cut out one cat.

3. Appliqués: Using the photo on page 89 as a guide, pin a cat and a fish to the pillow top. Appliqué, following Step 3 of the Cat & Fish Quilt (*page 88*).

4. Assembly: Stitch the 16-inch borders to the top and bottom edges of the pillow top, and the 15-inch borders to the side edges. With right sides facing, sew the pillow top to the pillow back around three sides and four corners, leaving an 8-inch opening on one side for turning. Clip the corners and turn the pillow right side out. Stuff the pillow and slipstitch the opening closed (*see Stitch Guide, page 146*).

AVERAGE:
For those with some experience in quilting.

DIMENSIONS:
About 14 x 19"

MATERIALS:
- 45-inch-wide fabric: ½ yard of green check; ⅓ yard each of small yellow check and yellow print
- synthetic stuffing
- ⅓ yard of lightweight fusible interfacing
- green sewing thread
- crisp cardboard or manila folders
- Basic Quilting Tools, page 137

FIG. III, 4B
FISH APPLIQUÉ PATTERN
FULL SIZE

THIS LITTLE PIGGY CRIB QUILT SET

THIS LITTLE PIGGY
CRIB QUILT SET

An adorable collection of pink piglets dancing across this quilt top and pillow make it a bright addition to a baby's room. Using a variety of prints and shades of pink fabric gives this set a unique look.

If you'd like a quilt of a different color, substitute other fabrics for some or all of the pink or white fabrics. Cut the appliqués from any color fabric—make them realistic or whimsical. For the background, use light blue, or try a neutral print, like yellow gingham or a white-based pindot. Be sure to choose fabrics with the same fiber content so the quilt may be cleaned easily. Read the tips for selecting quilt fabrics in the box on page 99 before beginning these projects.

THIS LITTLE PIGGY QUILT DIRECTIONS:
(¼-inch seams allowed)

1. Patterns: Enlarge the patterns in FIGS. III, 5A-5F (pages 94-99) onto paper, following the directions on page 145. The heavy lines are the outlines for the appliqué pieces and the dotted lines are underlaps or stitching lines. Make a separate pattern for each appliqué piece, and cut out the patterns.

2. Cutting: From white fabric, cut six 12 x 13-inch square blocks. **From dark pink print,** cut three 3½ x 48-inch strips, one 34½ x 47-inch quilt back and eight 3½ x 13-inch strips.

3. Appliqués: Arrange the assorted pink print fabrics into groups of light, medium and dark tones. Using the photo as a guide, and following the color keys in FIGS. 5A-5F, cut out the appliqué pieces from the assorted pink fabrics. Cut out complete pig figures from the solid pink fabric; the clothes or details will be appliquéd on top of the pig bodies. Pin the appliqué pieces to the white blocks following FIGS. 5A-5F, and overlapping the appliqué pieces as shown. Edgestitch around the appliqué pieces, then zigzag stitch over all the raw appliqué edges and on the dotted stitching lines.

4. Quilt Top: Using the photo as a placement guide, stitch a vertical row of three quilt blocks with 3½ x 13-inch strips between them, right sides together, beginning and ending with a pink strip. Repeat with the remaining quilt blocks and 13-inch strips. Stitch the block rows to either edge of a 3½ x 48-inch strip so all the pigs are facing the center strip. Stitch the remaining 3½ x 48-inch strips to the outer raw edges of the block rows. Trim the ends of all the strips flush with the top and bottom edges of the quilt blocks.

5. Assembly: Spread the quilt top, wrong side up, on a clean, flat surface, and tape down the corners. Place the batting on top of the quilt top. Starting at the center, working straight out to each edge and diagonally to each corner, baste through both layers. Trim the batting edges flush with the quilt top. Remove the tape, and turn the quilt top right side up. Place the quilt back, wrong side up, on the quilt top, and pin together all three layers. Stitch together all three layers around three sides

AVERAGE:
For those with some experience in quilting.

DIMENSIONS:
About 34 x 46"

MATERIALS:
- 45-inch-wide fabric: ⅔ yard of white; 2 yards of dark pink print (includes quilt back); ⅜ yard of solid pink; assorted scraps of light pink prints equivalent to ¾ yard; assorted scraps of medium and dark pink prints equivalent to ⅓ yard each
- matching sewing threads
- 36 x 48-inch piece of synthetic batting
- six-strand pink embroidery floss
- curved or darner needle
- paper for patterns
- tracing paper
- Basic Quilting Tools, page 137

SEAMLINE

FIG. III, 5A
FLYING PIGGY APPLIQUÉ PATTERN PIECES
1 SQ. = 1"

P = SOLID PINK
M = MEDIUM PINK
L = LIGHT PINK
D = DARK PINK

THIS
LITTLE
PIGGY CRIB
QUILT SET

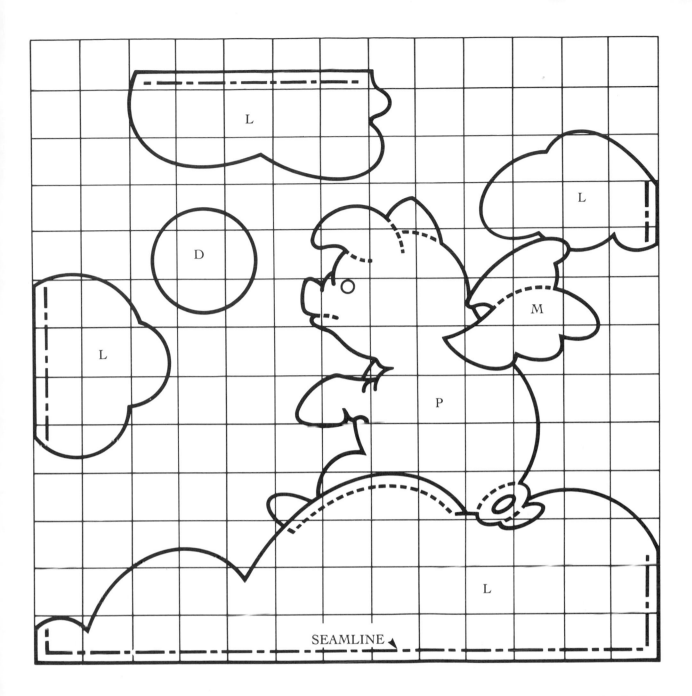

SEAMLINE ◄

and four corners, leaving an opening for turning on one side. Turn the quilt right side out. Remove the basting stitches, and slipstitch the opening closed (*see Stitch Guide, page 146*).

6. Tie-Quilting: Spread the quilt, right side up, on a clean, flat surface. Pin-baste through all three layers, placing a pin at each corner of a quilt block. Use a curved needle or a darner needle; a curved needle will make the stitching easier. Thread the needle with a length of the full (six strand)

pink embroidery floss; do not knot the floss. Starting at the center of the quilt, and working from the top, take a short stitch through all three layers at the corner of a quilt block; leave a 2-inch tail of floss. Take another stitch on top of the first. Cut the floss about 2 inches above the stitches. Tie the floss tails into a square knot (*see How To Tie A Square Knot, page 145*), and trim the ends to ½ inch. Repeat across the quilt, making ties at each corner of all the quilt blocks. Remove the basting pins.

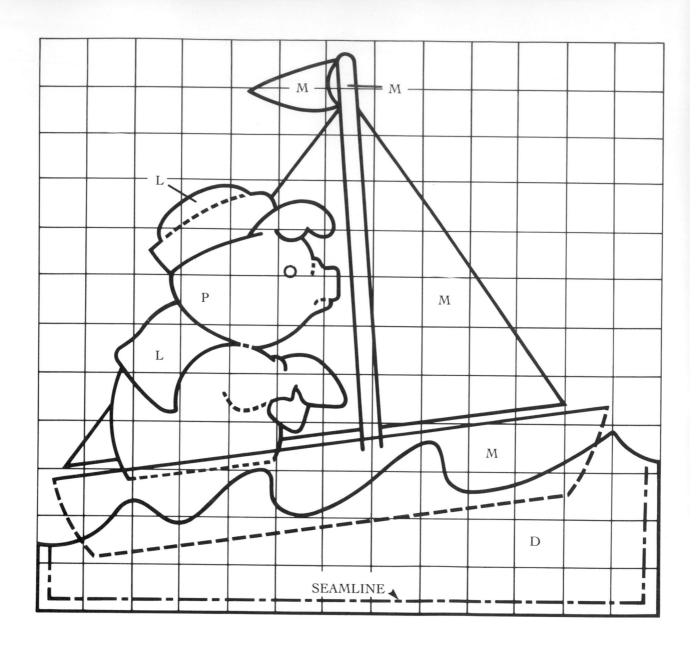

FIG. III, 5C
SAILING PIGGY APPLIQUÉ PATTERN PIECES
1 SQ. = 1"

P = SOLID PINK
M = MEDIUM PINK
L = LIGHT PINK
D = DARK PINK

THIS
LITTLE
PIGGY CRIB
QUILT SET

SEAMLINE

MATCHING FABRIC FIBERS

When choosing quilt fabrics from your scrap basket, be sure that all the fabrics used for a project have the same fiber content. This is important if you plan to wash the quilt.

To save time and insure a perfect match every time, mark fabric scraps before putting them in the scrap basket. Pin a label or lightly write the fiber content on the back of the scrap with a dressmaker's pencil or fabric marker.

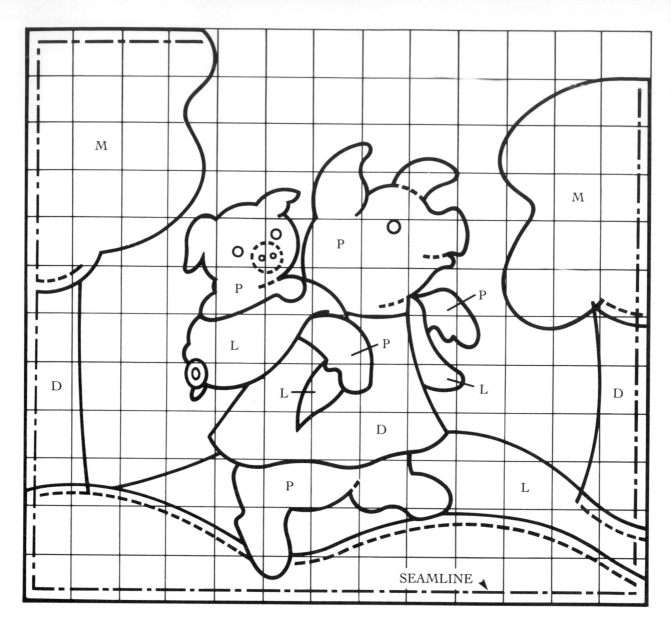

M

M

P

P

P

P

P

L

L

L

D

D

D

D

L

SEAMLINE ◄

FIG. III, 5E
MOTHER & BABY PIGGY APPLIQUÉ PATTERN PIECES
1 SQ. = 1"

P = SOLID PINK
M = MEDIUM PINK
L = LIGHT PINK
D = DARK PINK

THIS
LITTLE
PIGGY CRIB
QUILT SET

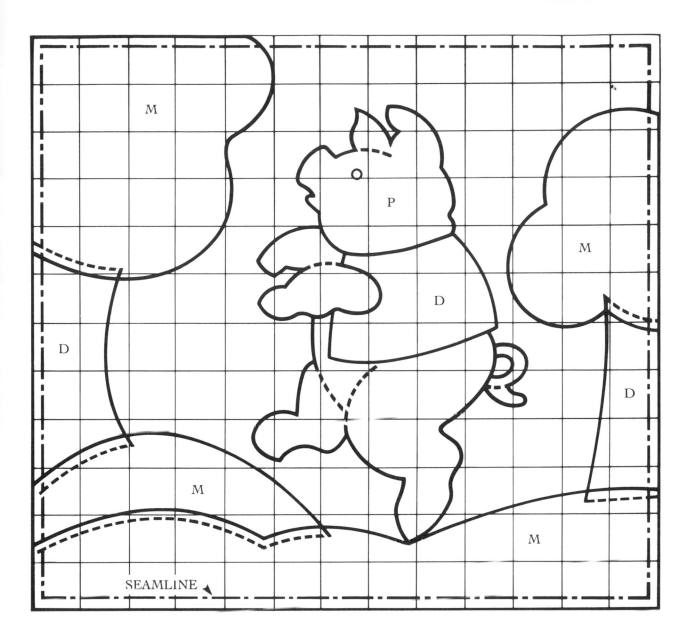

FIG. III, 5F
DANCING PIGGY APPLIQUÉ PATTERN PIECES
1 SQ. = 1″

THE QUILTER'S EYE

The ability to imagine a piece of printed fabric as part of a whole patchwork or appliqué motif is a learned skill. This "quilter's eye" is best developed by examining many quilts, old and new. Look closely at a quilt, then view it from a distance. This will allow you to see how the quilter used specific types, colors and patterns of fabrics to create the overall effect.

Look at printed fabrics not only for color but for the density of the print. For example, a white-based pindot usually has less density than a white-based calico because the pindots are smaller and spaced farther apart than the flowers on a calico. Although the fabrics may look similar on the bolt, as part of an entire quilt the pindot will create a lighter color effect than the calico.

Also consider the color of the print against the background color. For example, two calicos with the same slate blue background color — one with a white print and one with a black print. On the bolt, the fabrics may seem comparable, but in a patchwork motif the black print will make the slate blue appear darker.

THIS LITTLE PIGGY PILLOW

DIMENSIONS:
About 16 x 17"

MATERIALS:
- 45-inch-wide fabric:
  ⅓ yard of white;
  ½ yard of dark pink print;
  ⅛ yard of solid pink;
  assorted scraps of medium pink prints equivalent to ⅙ yard;
  assorted scraps of light pink prints equivalent to ⅟₇ yard;
  small scrap of dark pink print
- synthetic stuffing
- tracing paper
- Basic Quilting Tools, page 137

DIRECTIONS:
(¼-inch seams allowed)

1. Pattern: Enlarge the pattern in Fɪɢ. III, 5G following the directions on page 145. The heavy lines are the outlines for the appliqué pieces and the dotted lines are underlaps or stitching lines. Make a separate pattern for each appliqué piece, and cut out the patterns.

2. Cutting: From white fabric, cut one 12 x 13-inch square. **From dark pink print,** cut one 16 x 17-inch pillow back, two 2½ x 12-inch and two 2½ x 17-inch strips.

3. Appliqué: Using the photo on page 92 as a guide, and following the color key in Fɪɢ. III, 5G, cut out the pieces and appliqué following Step 3 of This Little Piggy Quilt (*page 93*).

4. Assembly: Stitch a 2½ x 12-inch strip to either side edge of the appliquéd square. Stitch a 2½ x 17-inch strip to the top and bottom edges of the square to complete the pillow top. With right sides facing, stitch the pillow back to the pillow top around three sides and four corners, leaving an opening on one side for turning. Turn the pillow right side out and stuff it firmly. Turn in the open edges and slipstitch the opening closed (*see Stitch Guide, page 146*).

FIG. III, 5G
SLEEPING PIGGY PILLOW APPLIQUÉ PATTERN PIECES
1 SQ. = 1"

P = SOLID PINK
M = MEDIUM PINK
L = LIGHT PINK
D = DARK PINK

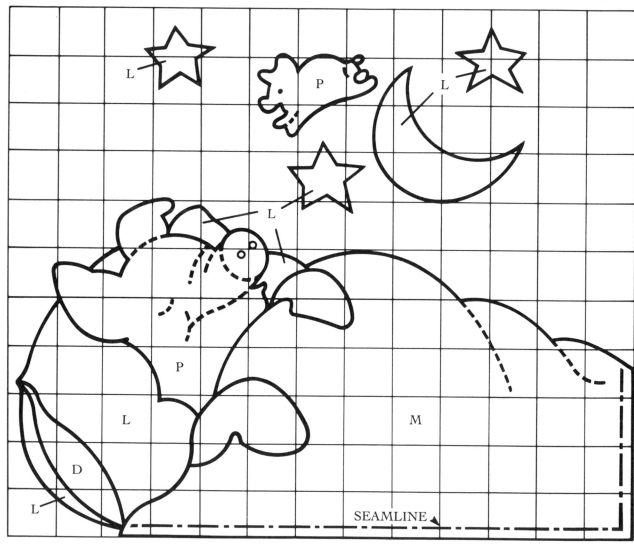

BOWS AND LACE CARRIAGE SET

This pretty set is extremely easy to make, and is the perfect size for a carriage or stroller. Bows and Lace Carriage Set (directions, page 102) is made from sturdy, washable navy blue broadcloth, so it can stand up to everyday use. The coverlet has dozens of tiny satin bows tacked over it — no hand-quilting necessary. Be sure to stitch the bows securely so baby can't pull them off.

Since babies don't usually sleep with pillows, place this one at the head of the carriage as a cushion, or on a nursery rocking chair to make those late night visits more comfortable.

EASY:
Achievable by anyone.

DIMENSIONS:
About 33 x 38"

MATERIALS:
- 2 yards of 45-inch-wide navy blue broadcloth
- 3¼ yards of 1⅜-inch-wide white beaded eyelet lace
- 3¼ yards of ¼-inch-wide pink satin ribbon
- 4¼ yards of ⅛-inch-wide pink satin ribbon
- matching sewing threads
- 35 x 40-inch piece of synthetic batting
- white dressmaker's pencil
- Basic Quilting Tools, page 137

BOWS AND LACE COVERLET DIRECTIONS:

1. Cutting: From the blue broadcloth, cut one 33 x 38-inch coverlet top and one 35½ x 40½-inch coverlet back. **From the white beaded eyelet lace,** cut two 15-inch lengths and two 40-inch lengths. **From the ¼-inch-wide pink satin ribbon,** cut two 15-inch lengths and two 40-inch lengths. **From the ⅛-inch-wide pink satin ribbon,** cut forty-two 3½-inch lengths.

2. Quilt Top: Spread the coverlet top, right side up, on a clean, flat surface, and tape down the corners. With the white dressmaker's pencil, mark points along the top and side edges 10 inches from the upper right-hand corner of the coverlet top. Using a yardstick, draw a diagonal line to connect the marks. Mark points on the top and side edges of the coverlet top 12 inches beyond the first marks, and connect the second marks with a diagonal line. Repeat, measuring from the lower left-hand corner, to make two more diagonal lines. Thread the ¼-inch ribbon lengths through the corresponding lengths of beaded eyelet lace. Pin the lace/ribbons, centered, over each drawn diagonal line. Remove the tape. Sew the lace/ribbons in place by edgestitching along both sides of the ribbons, not the lace.

3. Basting: Turn each edge of the coverlet back ¼ inch to the wrong side of the fabric, and press in place. Spread the coverlet back, wrong side up, on a clean, flat surface, and tape down the corners. Place the batting, centered, on top of the coverlet back. Place the coverlet top, right side up and centered, on top of the batting. Starting at the center, working straight out to each edge and diagonally out to each corner, pin through all three layers of the quilt. Remove the tape. Fold one long side edge of the coverlet back over the batting and pin it to the coverlet top 1 inch in from the top's raw edges. Using a wide zigzag stitch, sew the folded edge of the coverlet back to the coverlet top through all three layers. Repeat for the remaining three edges of the coverlet.

4. Finishing: Make each length of the ⅛-inch-wide ribbon into a knotless bow by folding the ribbon into two loops and tying them in the center with a piece of thread. Pin the bows to the coverlet through all three layers, placing the bows in rows parallel to the lace/ribbons. Stitch the bows in place through their centers, taking several stitches through all three layers to securely anchor the bows.

TYING AND TACKING

In days gone by, quilts used during the cold winter months were made with an extra layer or two of batting inside. The additional thickness of the quilt made it difficult for the quilter to hand-stitch through all the layers. Instead, quilters used tie-quilting (*see Water Lily Quilt, page 40*) or tacking (*see Bows and Lace Carriage Set, page 101*). Both of these methods require just a few stitches, evenly placed over the surface of the quilt, to hold together the quilt top, batting and back. Traditionally, tacking was not especially decorative. To dress up the tacking on the Bows and Lace Coverlet, the stitching is done through small satin ribbon bows.

BOWS AND LACE PILLOW

DIRECTIONS:

1. Cutting: From the blue broadcloth, cut two 10½ x 14½-inch pieces for the pillow top and back, and one 3¼ x 90-inch strip, pieced as needed, for the ruffle. **From the ⅛-inch-wide pink satin ribbon,** cut two 15-inch lengths, two 11-inch lengths and one 28-inch length. **From the ¼-inch-wide pink satin ribbon,** cut one 15-inch length, one 11-inch length and one 2½-yard length.

2. Pillow Top: Place the pillow top on a clean, flat surface, and tape down the corners. Pin a ⅛ x 15-inch ribbon across the pillow top, 1¾ inches from the long, top edge. Pin a ¼ x 15-inch ribbon ¼ inch below and parallel to the first ribbon, and pin a ⅛ x 15-inch ribbon ¼ inch below and parallel to the second ribbon. Edgestitch all the ribbons in place. Repeat with the 11-inch-long ribbons starting 1¾ inches from the left side edge of the pillow top (*see photo, page 101*). Tie the 28-inch length of ribbon in a knotless bow following Bows and Lace Coverlet, Step 4 (*page 102*), and stitch the bow securely to the pillow top where the ribbons meet.

3. Ruffle: Turn under one long edge of the ruffle strip ¼ inch to the wrong side of the fabric. Press the folded edge, turn it ¼ inch again, and stitch the hem. Thread the 2½ yards of ¼-inch-wide pink satin ribbon through the beaded eyelet lace. Stitch the lace/ribbon to the ruffle strip, placing it about ⅜ inch from the hemmed edge, and stitch along both edges of the ribbon. Stitch together the short ends of the ruffle, right sides together, to make a loop. Stitch two gathering rows ¼ inch and ½ inch from the long raw edge of the ruffle loop. With right sides together and raw edges even, pin the ruffle to the pillow top around all four sides. Pull up the gathering threads until the ruffle fits the pillow top, distributing the gathers evenly. Machine baste the ruffle to the pillow top, stitching about ¼ inch from the raw edges. Fold the ruffle toward the center of the pillow top. With right sides together and raw edges even, pin the pillow back to the pillow top with the ruffle between them. Stitch around three sides and four corners, stitching through all three layers and leaving an opening on one side. Turn the pillow right side out, stuff it firmly and slipstitch the opening closed (*see Stitch Guide, page 146*).

EASY:
Achievable by anyone.

DIMENSIONS:
About 9½ x 13½″

MATERIALS:
- 1 yard of 45-inch-wide navy blue broadcloth
- 2½ yards of 1⅜-inch-wide white beaded eyelet lace
- 3½ yards of ¼-inch-wide pink satin ribbon
- 2½ yards of ⅛-inch-wide pink satin ribbon
- synthetic stuffing
- Basic Quilting Tools, page 137

 BABY-COLORED COVERS

Traditionally, quilts and coverlets made for babies in the 19th century often were made from pure white fabric decorated only with quilt stitching. Today many folks still favor all-white or pastel colored layettes for newborns.

To give the Bows and Lace Carriage Set a softer, more traditional look, substitute pale blue, pink or yellow fabric for the navy blue broadcloth suggested, and use white or matching ribbon bows. Or, try white fabric with multicolored pastel ribbon bows. If the coverlet will be used as a christening blanket, use white fabric and decorate the coverlet with white bows and lace.

SAILBOAT QUILT

Sailboat Quilt brings both sunlight and sweet dreams to the nursery. This colorful quilt makes a wonderful wall-hanging or can brighten up any bed, and the simple sun/sea/boat appliqués are a joy for a child's eyes.

A perfect project for those who want to hone their skills, Sailboat Quilt is machine-quilted one block at a time, then assembled. The appliqués are relatively simple to cut and piece, and the detail stitching is not complicated at all. To complete the quilt, each block is tufted, or tacked, and trimmed with jaunty red yarn.

For a softer version of the Sailboat quilt, use a pale blue fabric for the sky, pale yellow for the sun, and a pastel or light print for the boat.

■

AVERAGE:
For those with some experience in quilting.

DIMENSIONS:
About 36 x 48"

MATERIALS:
- 45-inch-wide fabric:
  1⅓ yards each of blue and white ticking and plain muslin;
  1⅞ yards of blue;
  1 yard of red;
  ⅕ yard of yellow;
  ½ yard of opaque white
- 52 x 72-inch piece of bonded synthetic batting
- red and blue sewing threads
- red 4-ply yarn
- tracing paper
- crisp cardboard or manila folders
- glue stick
- white fabric marking pencil
- Basic Quilting Tools, page 137

DIRECTIONS:
(½-inch seams allowed)

1. Patterns: Trace the full-sized pattern in Fig. III, 6A *(page 106)* onto tracing paper. Make two sail patterns, one with and one without clouds. Make full patterns of the half patterns in Figs. III, 6B-6C *(page 107)*: fold the tracing paper in half, place the paper fold along the dotted pattern line and trace the half pattern. Cut out the folded half pattern and open it for a full pattern. Glue the tracing paper patterns to the crisp cardboard or manila folders, and cut out the patterns. Also draw and cut out a 5-inch-diameter circle from cardboard.

2. Cutting: From blue and white ticking, cut nine 12 x 16-inch squares with the stripes running lengthwise. **From muslin,** cut nine 12 x 16-inch quilt block backing pieces. **From white fabric,** cut five sails without clouds and four sails with clouds. **From blue fabric,** cut one 40 x 52-inch quilt back and nine seas. **From yellow fabric,** cut five circles for suns. **From red fabric,** cut nine boats and four 5½ x 44-inch borders. **From batting,** cut pieces to match the ticking squares and red borders.

3. Appliqués: Using the photo as a guide, pin the sea appliqués to the ticking squares matching the side and bottom edges. Slide a boat, centered, ¼ inch under each sea *(see dotted line in Fig. III, 6C)*, and pin in place. Edgestitch around the appliqués. On four squares, pin the sails with clouds, centered, ¼ inch above the boats. Edgestitch around the appliqué, and along the lines separating the two sails and the sails and clouds *(see dotted lines in Fig. III, 6A)*. Cut away the white fabric between the two sails. On the five remaining squares, pin and edgestitch the sails without clouds, and pin and edgestitch a sun to the upper left-hand corner. The sun will extend beyond the top and left side edges of the square *(see photo)*. Using a ruler and the fabric pencil, and the photo as a guide, draw five rays from each sun.

4. Quilting: Place a muslin block on a clean, flat surface, and place a batting piece, centered, on top of the muslin. Place an appliquéd block on top of the batting, and pin baste all three layers together. To quilt the block, machine satin stitch over all the stitching lines, drawn lines and appliqué edges, stitching

(Continued on page 106)

SAILBOAT QUILT

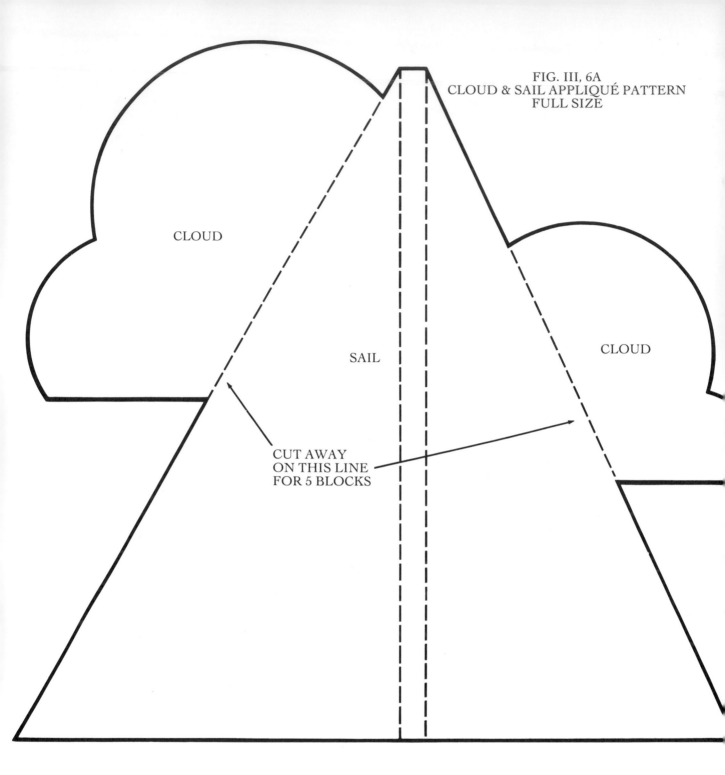

CLOUD

SAIL

CLOUD

CUT AWAY
ON THIS LINE
FOR 5 BLOCKS

through all three layers. Repeat with the remaining blocks.

5. Assembly: On the back of each quilt block, draw a line 1½ inches from each edge, starting with a line parallel to the bottom edge of the block. The finished drawn rectangle should measure 9 x 13 inches. Trim the edges of the quilt blocks until they are ½ inch from the drawn lines. With right sides together, stitch a "cloud" block between two "sun" blocks

along their long edges. Repeat to make a second sun/cloud/sun row. Stitch together the remaining quilt blocks to make a cloud/sun/cloud row. With right sides facing and seams matching, stitch together the quilt block rows placing the cloud/sun/cloud row in the center.

6. Border: Stitch a red border to either side edge of the quilt block assembly. Trim the border ends flush with the quilt top. Stitch the remaining borders to the top and bottom edges of the assembly. Trim the border's ends flush with the far edges of the side borders. Baste the batting strips to the wrong sides of the border strips.

7. Finishing: Pin-baste the quilt top to the quilt back, right sides together. Stitch the quilt top to the back around three sides and four corners, leaving an opening on the top edge. Trim the corners, turn the quilt right side out, and slipstitch the opening closed (*see Stitch Guide, page 146*).

8. Tie-Quilting: Cut thirty-two 4-inch-long pieces of yarn. Spread the quilt, right side up, on a clean, flat surface. Pin-baste through all three layers at each corner of a quilt block. Knot one end of strong blue sewing thread. Starting at the center of the quilt, and working from the top, take a stitch at one of the pins. Place two pieces of yarn at the stitch point, and take two more stitches over the center of the yarn. Fasten the thread on the quilt back. Tie the yarn ends in a square knot (*see How To Tie A Square Knot, page 115*), and trim the ends. Repeat at the remaining pins.

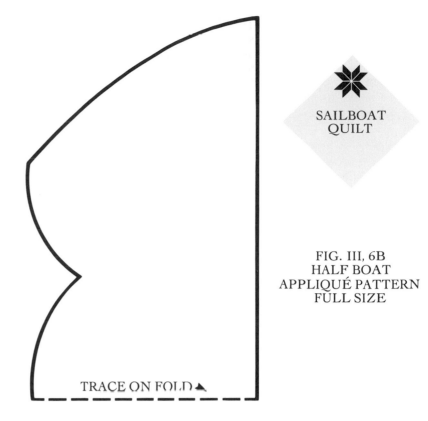

SAILBOAT QUILT

FIG. III, 6B
HALF BOAT
APPLIQUÉ PATTERN
FULL SIZE

TRACE ON FOLD ▲

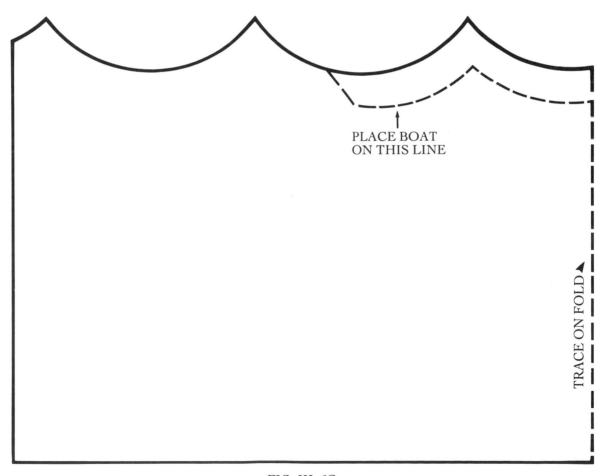

PLACE BOAT
ON THIS LINE

TRACE ON FOLD ▲

FIG. III, 6C
HALF SEA PATTERN
FULL SIZE

PILLOWS AND OTHER EXTRAS

THE PROJECTS IN THIS CHAPTER ALLOW THE LESS-EXPERIENCED STITCHER TO TRY OUT VARIOUS TECHNIQUES BEFORE ATTEMPTING A QUILT. BY PRACTICING CUTTING AND PIECING PATCHES ON THESE SMALLER ITEMS, YOU CAN GAIN THE SKILLS NEEDED TO MAKE MORE COMPLICATED PROJECTS.

EXPERT QUILTERS WHO ARE INTERESTED IN LEARNING A NEW TECHNIQUE CAN TRY TRAPUNTO OR FOLDED-FABRIC PATCHWORK. FOR A REAL CRAFTING CHALLENGE, TRY OUR GREENHOUSE PILLOWS: THE PILLOW FRONTS ARE PAINTED, THEN THE PAINTED PIECES ARE QUILTED TO CREATE A WONDERFULLY TEXTURED EFFECT.

BRING A BIT OF PATCHWORK INTO ANY ROOM IN THE HOUSE WITH A COLORFUL TABLE RUNNER, OR ANY OF THE PRETTY PILLOWS IN THIS CHAPTER. MANY OF THESE PROJECTS CAN BE MADE IN AN EVENING — PERFECT FOR GIFT-GIVING.

USE THESE PROJECTS AS A STARTING POINT TO BUILD YOUR SKILLS. THEN ADAPT SOME OF THESE ITEMS INTO LARGER AND MORE ELABORATE PIECES.

CHAPTER 4

AMISH ROSE & SWISS LILY PILLOWS
(directions, pages 110-112 and 113-114)

AMISH ROSE PILLOW

CHALLENGING:
Requires more
experience in quilting.

DIMENSIONS:
About 14″ square,
without ruffle

MATERIALS:
- 45-inch-wide cotton:
  ½ yard of white print;
  ¼ yard each of light
  blue print and dark
  blue print
- 6½-inch square of
  pre-printed fabric for
  center motif
- 15-inch square
  of muslin
- white and blue
  sewing threads
- blue quilting thread
- ¾ yard of lace trim
- 15-inch square
  of batting
- 1⅔ yards of ⅛-inch
  cording
- 12-inch white zipper
- 14-inch-square
  pillow form
- quilting hoop
- crisp cardboard
  or manila folders
- Basic Quilting Tools,
  page 137

The Amish Rose Pillow and the Swiss Lily Pillow (directions, page 113) shown in the photo on pages 108-109 are created with pre-printed decorative fabric squares surrounded by calico patchwork. An original design of embroidery, fabric painting or quilt stitching may be substituted for the center fabric motif. If the pillows are to be a gift, embroider or appliqué the recipient's name or initials on the center panel. As a set or individually, these country-style pillows make lovely gifts.

The patchwork on these pillows doesn't require a great deal of fabric, so they are perfect projects to use up scraps left over from a quilt or sewing project. Because the patches are so small, the piecing can be a little tricky; remember to begin and end the stitching ¼ inch from the raw edges of the patches to allow room for joining. The Amish Rose pillow is finished with a ruffle and the Swiss Lily is finished with a corded edge.

DIRECTIONS:
(¼-inch seams allowed, except where noted)

1. Pattern: Trace the full-size patterns in FIG. IV, 1A onto the crisp cardboard or manila folders, making a separate pattern for each lettered patch. Transfer the letters to the patterns, and cut out the patterns. The arrows in FIG. IV, 1A indicate the direction of the fabric print; transfer the arrows to the patterns.

2. Cutting: On the wrong side of the fabric, carefully trace around the patterns with a sharp, soft-lead pencil and transfer the arrows and letters. Cut out each patch ¼ inch beyond the pencil lines for the seam allowance. The pencil line is the stitchline. **From the white print fabric,** cut eight B, four D and four F patches, four 4 x 18-inch ruffle strips, pieced together to make a ruffle strip 72 inches long, and two 8½ x 16-inch pillow backs. **From the light blue print fabric,** cut four C and four A patches, and a 1½ x 60-inch bias strip, pieced as needed. **From the dark blue print fabric,** cut four E and four G patches.

3. Patchwork: To assemble the patchwork corners, follow FIG. IV, 1B, Steps 1-5 *(page 112)*, and refer to the photo on pages 108-109. When stitching together the patches, begin and end the stitching ¼ inch from the raw edges to allow room for joining; the raw edges of the patches will not match, but the stitchlines will. With right sides together, stitch together an A and a B patch, a C and a D patch, and a B and a G patch *(see Step 1)*. Stitch an E patch to the A/B assembly, and an F patch to the C/D assembly *(see Step 2)*. Stitch together the B/G and the C/D/F assemblies *(see Step 3)*, then add the A/B/E assembly *(see Step 4)*. Repeat with the remaining patches to make three more corner assemblies. Stitch together the four corner assemblies following Step 5. Press all the seams open.

4. Center Square: Fold the pre-printed fabric square in quarters to find the center point, and mark the center point. On the wrong side of the fabric, mark a square 3 inches from the center point on all four sides. Stitch the center square to the patchwork assembly, one side at a time. Press the seams towards the patchwork.

5. Quilting: Spread the muslin square on a clean, flat surface and place the batting, centered, on top of the muslin. Place the

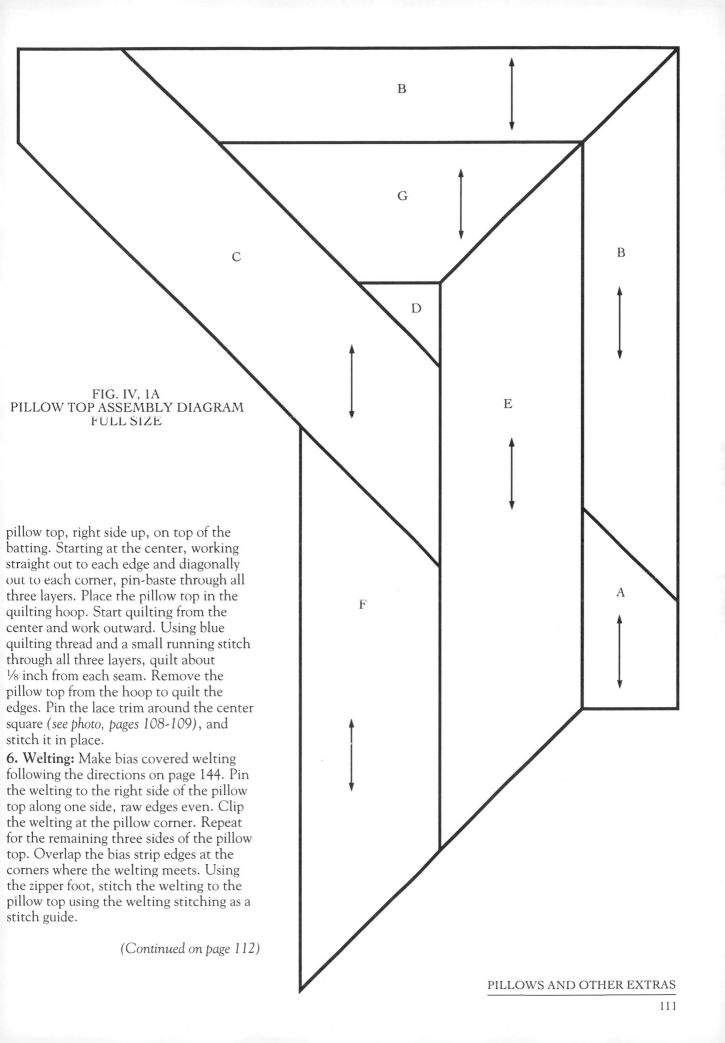

FIG. IV, 1A
PILLOW TOP ASSEMBLY DIAGRAM
FULL SIZE

pillow top, right side up, on top of the batting. Starting at the center, working straight out to each edge and diagonally out to each corner, pin-baste through all three layers. Place the pillow top in the quilting hoop. Start quilting from the center and work outward. Using blue quilting thread and a small running stitch through all three layers, quilt about ⅛ inch from each seam. Remove the pillow top from the hoop to quilt the edges. Pin the lace trim around the center square (*see photo, pages 108-109*), and stitch it in place.

6. Welting: Make bias covered welting following the directions on page 144. Pin the welting to the right side of the pillow top along one side, raw edges even. Clip the welting at the pillow corner. Repeat for the remaining three sides of the pillow top. Overlap the bias strip edges at the corners where the welting meets. Using the zipper foot, stitch the welting to the pillow top using the welting stitching as a stitch guide.

(*Continued on page 112*)

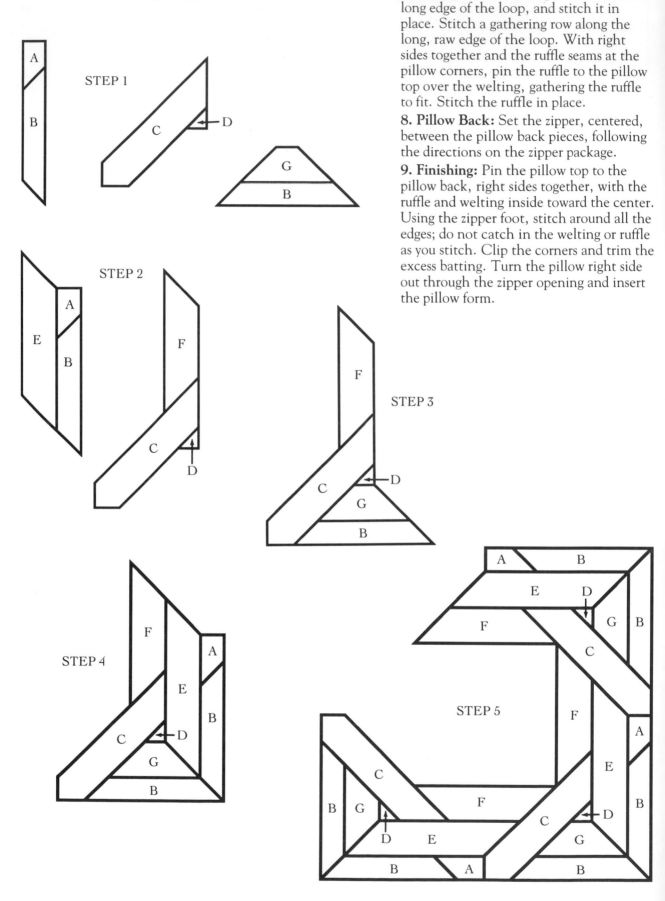

7. Ruffle: Stitch together the ends of the ruffle strip to make a loop. Turn under one long edge of the loop, and stitch it in place. Stitch a gathering row along the long, raw edge of the loop. With right sides together and the ruffle seams at the pillow corners, pin the ruffle to the pillow top over the welting, gathering the ruffle to fit. Stitch the ruffle in place.

8. Pillow Back: Set the zipper, centered, between the pillow back pieces, following the directions on the zipper package.

9. Finishing: Pin the pillow top to the pillow back, right sides together, with the ruffle and welting inside toward the center. Using the zipper foot, stitch around all the edges; do not catch in the welting or ruffle as you stitch. Clip the corners and trim the excess batting. Turn the pillow right side out through the zipper opening and insert the pillow form.

SWISS LILY PILLOW

(photo, pages 108-109)

DIRECTIONS:
(¼-inch seams allowed)

1. Patterns: Trace the full-size patterns in FIG. IV, 2A *(page 114)* onto the crisp cardboard or manila folders, making a separate pattern for each triangle and the square. Cut out the patterns.

2. Cutting: On the wrong side of the fabric, carefully trace around the patterns with a sharp, soft-lead pencil. Cut out each patch ¼ inch beyond the pencil lines for the seam allowance. The pencil line is the stitchline. **From the white fabric,** cut 8 squares, 8 small triangles and 4 large triangles. Flop the pattern and cut 4 more large triangles. Also cut two 8½ x 16-inch pillow back pieces. **From the red fabric,** cut 8 large triangles, flop the pattern and cut 8 more large triangles. Also cut a 2 x 60-inch bias strip, pieced as needed. **From the purple fabric,** cut 8 small triangles and 4 large triangles. Flop the pattern and cut 4 more large triangles.

3. Patchwork: To assemble the patchwork corners, follow FIG. IV, 2B, Steps 1-3 *(page 114)*. With right sides together, stitch a small white triangle to a small purple triangle along their long edges. Repeat to make a total of 8 white/purple squares. In the same way, stitch together the large triangles to make 8 red/white rectangles and 8 red/purple rectangles *(see Step 1)*. Stitch a white square to one purple edge of each white/purple square. Stitch together pairs of the red/purple rectangles along their short red edges. Stitch together pairs of the red/white rectangles along their short white edges. Stitch a red/purple rectangle to a red/white rectangle along their long purple and red edges. Repeat to make three more double rectangles *(see Step 2)*. Following Step 3, stitch together pairs of the square assemblies to make four pieced squares, and stitch a pieced square to one short end of the four double rectangles. To assemble the patchwork, stitch the square/rectangle assemblies together, placing them at right angles, matching the short end of the rectangle to the top raw edge of the square. Press the seams open.

4. Center Square: Fold the pre-printed fabric square in quarters to find the center point, and mark the center point. On the wrong side of the fabric, mark a square 3 inches from the center point on all four sides. Stitch the center square to the patchwork assembly, one side at a time. Press the seams towards the patchwork.

5. Quilting: Spread the muslin square on a clean, flat surface, and place the batting, centered, on top of the muslin. Place the pillow top, right side up, on top of the batting. Starting at the center, working straight out to each edge and diagonally out to each corner, pin-baste through all three layers. Place the pillow top in the quilting hoop. Start quilting from the center and work outward. Using red quilting thread and a small running stitch through all three layers, quilt about ⅛ inch from each seam. Remove the pillow top from the hoop to quilt the edges. Pin the lace trim around the center square *(see photo, pages 108-109)*, and stitch it in place.

6. Welting: Make bias covered welting following the directions on page 144. Pin the welting to the right side of the pillow top along one side, raw edges even. Clip the welting at the pillow corner. Repeat for the remaining three sides of the pillow top. Overlap the bias strip edges at the corners where the welting meets. Using the zipper foot, stitch the welting to the pillow top using the welting stitching as a stitch guide.

7. Pillow Back: Set the zipper, centered, between the pillow back pieces, following the directions on the zipper package.

8. Finishing: Pin the pillow top to the pillow back, right sides together, with the welting inside toward the center. Using the zipper foot, stitch around all the edges; do not catch in the welting as you stitch. Clip the corners and trim the excess batting. Turn the pillow right side out through the zipper opening and insert the pillow form.

AVERAGE:
For those with some experience in patchwork.

DIMENSIONS:
About 14" square

MATERIALS:

- 45-inch-wide cotton: ½ yard of white; ¼ yard each of purple and red
- 6½-inch square of pre-printed fabric for center motif
- 15-inch square of muslin
- ¾ yard of lace trim
- white and red sewing threads
- red quilting thread
- 1⅔ yards of ¼-inch cording
- 12-inch white zipper
- 15-inch square of batting
- 14-inch-square pillow form
- crisp cardboard or manila folders
- quilting hoop
- Basic Quilting Tools, page 137

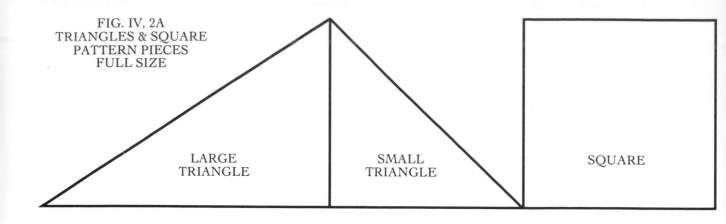

LARGE
TRIANGLE

SMALL
TRIANGLE

SQUARE

FIG. IV, 2B
PILLOW TOP PIECING DIAGRAM

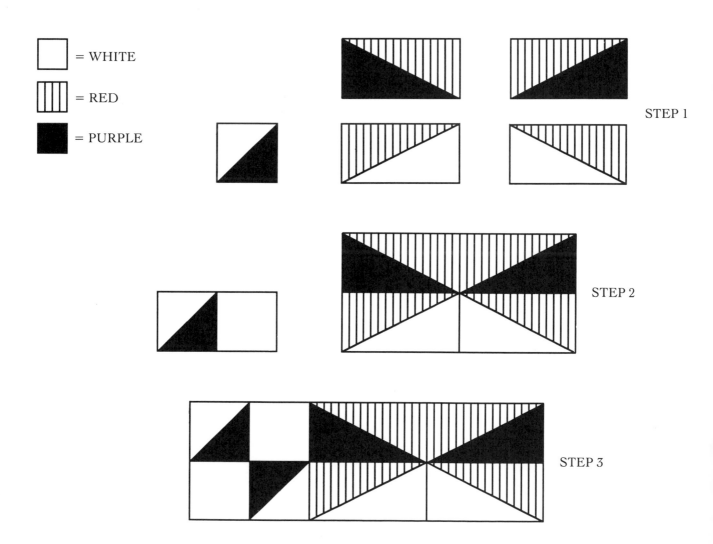

= WHITE

= RED

= PURPLE

STEP 1

STEP 2

STEP 3

GREENHOUSE PILLOWS

Bring the blooming beauty of spring into your home with this lovely set of Greenhouse Pillows (directions, pages 116-119). *These unusual pillows actually are made from simple muslin squares which are painted, including the background "patchwork" grids. The vividly colored designs then are quilted to give the flat pictures texture and to add visual interest.*

When trying out a new crafting technique, a pillow is a wonderful place to start. Combining old and new techniques to make these pillows places them in the best tradition of American crafting.

■

AVERAGE:
For those with some experience in patchwork.

DIMENSIONS:
Square pillow is about 16″ square; rectangular pillow is about 14 x 18″

MATERIALS:
To make five pillows:
- Ballpoint paint tubes: red, yellow, light blue, green, white, light green, violet, rust, tan, brown, rose
- matching sewing threads
- black quilting thread
- 4½ yards of 45-inch-wide muslin
- 72 x 90-inches of synthetic batting
- synthetic stuffing or pillow forms
- tracing paper
- dressmaker's carbon
- stylus or dry ballpoint pen
- large quilting hoop, or a large square of corrugated cardboard and thumbtacks
- lint-free cloth
- cleaning fluid
- Basic Quilting Tools, page 137

R = RED
G = GREEN
T = TAN
W = WHITE
P = PLAIN
LB = LIGHT BLUE
Y = YELLOW

GREENHOUSE PILLOWS GENERAL DIRECTIONS:

1. To hold the fabric taut for painting, place it in the large quilting hoop or stretch it over the corrugated cardboard, tacking the fabric in place.

2. To paint, hold the paint tube vertically as you would a pen. Bear down on the fabric with the tube and rub on the color as you would with wax crayons.

3. Wipe the tip of the paint tube frequently with the lint-free cloth to keep the tip from clogging.

4. To correct mistakes, promptly wipe the fabric with the cleaning fluid.

5. Let the painted fabric dry for at least 48 hours before washing, dry-cleaning or ironing it. Otherwise the painted fabric can be worked with after eight hours.

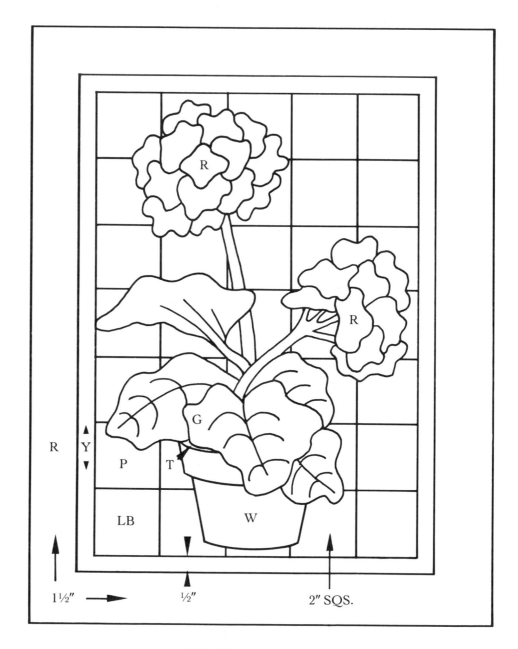

FIG. IV, 3A GERANIUM

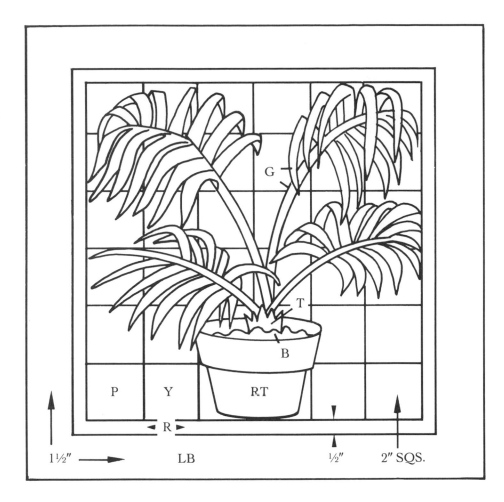

G = GREEN
T = TAN
B = BROWN
RT = RUST
P = PLAIN
Y = YELLOW
R = RED
LB = LIGHT BLUE

FIG. IV, 3B   PALM

DIRECTIONS:

1. Patterns: Enlarge the designs in FIGS. IV, 3A-3E *(pages 116-119)* onto tracing paper, following the directions on page 145. Include the grid lines in pattern; they will form the "patchwork" background.

2. Cutting: For each square pillow, cut three 19-inch square pieces of muslin. For each rectangular pillow, cut three 17 x 21-inch pieces of muslin. For each pillow, cut three pieces of batting the same size as the muslin pieces.

3. Pillow Top: For each pillow top, spread one piece of muslin on a clean, flat surface. Place pieces of tape at each corner and around all the edges to hold the muslin taut. Place the dressmaker's carbon, colored side down, on top of the muslin. Center the tracing paper pattern on top of the dressmaker's carbon. Using the stylus or dry ballpoint pen, carefully trace over all the lines of the pattern to transfer the design to the muslin. Following the General Directions and FIGS. IV, 3A-3E, and using the photo on page 115 as a guide, paint the "patchwork" background grid design with the ballpoint paint tubes. Carefully paint the plant and container. Let the paint dry for at least eight hours.

4. Quilting: When the paint has dried completely, spread a plain piece of muslin on a clean, flat surface, and tape down the corners. Place three pieces of batting on top of the muslin. Place a painted pillow top, centered, on top of the batting. Starting at the center, working straight out to each edge and diagonally out to each corner, baste through all three layers. Remove the tape. Place the pillow top in the quilting hoop. Start quilting from the center and work outward. Using the black

If a quilting project
has an elaborate
color scheme or a
detailed appliqué,
patch or, as in the
Greenhouse Pillows,
painted design, the
choice of a quilting
design is very easy.
The more elaborate
the other elements
of a quilt are, the
simpler the stitching
should be. But if the
quilt is simple, the
stitching can be as
elaborate as you
like. Finding new
quilting designs is
quite easy, as almost
any kind of pattern
can be used. Stencil
patterns are ideal, as
are many patterns
designed for cut-
paper silhouettes.
Children's coloring
books often can
provide inspired
designs for a child's
quilt. Many
appliqué patterns
can be transformed
into quilting
patterns, and even a
pretty wallpaper
design can be
simplified for
stitching.

quilting thread and a small running stitch,
quilt over all the pattern lines. If you wish,
machine-quilt through all three layers over
all the pattern lines, backstitching over
the ends of the thread to secure them.
When the quilting is finished, remove the
basting threads.

5. Finishing: Place the remaining piece of
muslin, right side up, on a clean, flat
surface. Place the quilted pillow top,
wrong side up and raw edges matching, on
top of the plain muslin, and pin the pieces
together through all the layers. Stitch
together the pillow top and back, 1½
inches from the raw edges, around three
sides and four corners, leaving an opening
on one side for turning. Clip the corners
and trim the seam allowance to ½ inch.
Turn the pillow right side out and stuff the
pillow or insert the pillow form. Turn in
the open edges and slipstitch the opening
closed (*see Stitch Guide, page 146*).

RO = ROSE
V = VIOLET
LG = LIGHT GREEN
HG = LEAF HIGHLIGHTS
T = TAN
RT = RUST
P = PLAIN
LB = LIGHT BLUE
Y = YELLOW

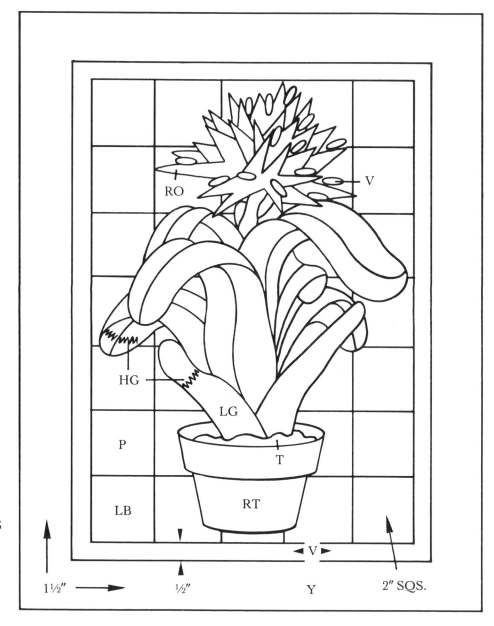

FIG. IV, 3C BROMELIAD

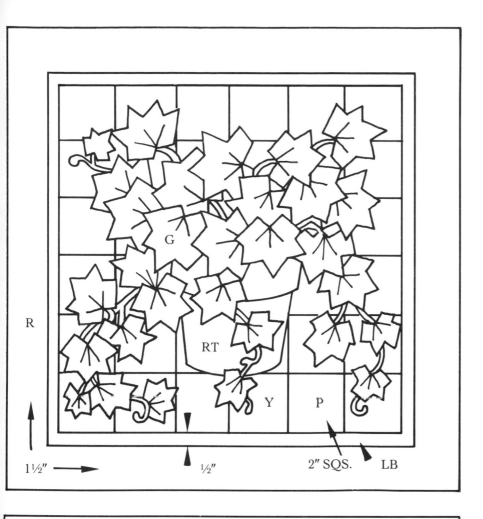

FIG. IV, 3D
IVY

G = GREEN
RT = RUST
Y = YELLOW
P = PLAIN
LB = LIGHT BLUE
R = RED

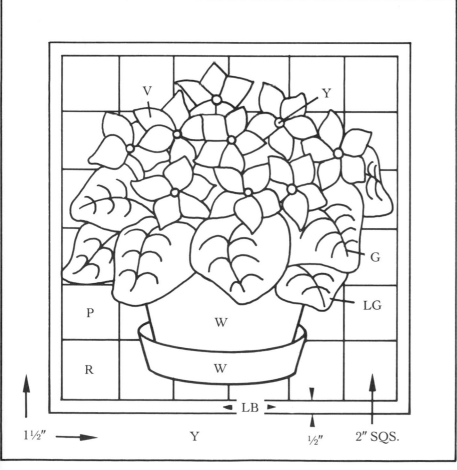

FIG. IV, 3E
AFRICAN VIOLET

V = VIOLET
Y = YELLOW
G = GREEN
LG = LIGHT GREEN
W = WHITE
P = PLAIN
R = RED
LB = LIGHT BLUE

PILLOWS AND OTHER EXTRAS

119

QUILTED SATIN BOUDOIR SET

This lovely set in ivory satin recalls the Victorian era, when clever needlewomen used the practical art of quilting purely for decorative purposes. Examples of decorative quilting can be found on any number of personal items, including fancy petticoats and corset covers. This Boudoir Set would make a perfect Mother's Day present, or a lovely shower gift for the bride-to-be.

An experienced quilter can make these projects in a few hours. A quilting hoop is essential to hold the slippery satin in place as you stitch. For a different look, substitute a pretty pink or blue satin, or a rich burgundy or forest green satin. Use either matching or contrasting color thread for the quilting.

PILLOW DIRECTIONS:
(⅝-inch seams allowed)

1. Cutting: From satin, cut two 14-inch- and one 2½-inch-diameter circles and two 6 x 45-inch strips. **From batting,** cut two 14-inch-diameter circles. **From muslin,** cut one 14-inch-diameter circle.

2. Quilting: Fold a large satin circle in half twice to find and mark the center. Using the dressmaker's pencil and a ruler, draw lines radiating out from the center across the circle. Insert the dressmaker's pencil into a compass. Place the point of the compass on the center mark and draw a 1½-inch-diameter circle. Place a muslin circle on a flat surface. Place a batting circle and the marked satin circle, right side up, on top. Pin-baste all three layers together. Place the pillow top in the hoop. Starting from the center and using small running stitches, quilt over the straight marked lines through all three layers.

3. Lace Trim: Pin the straight edge of a 40-inch piece of lace ⅝ inch from the edges of the pillow top. Turn under the lace ends, and stitch in place. Hand-sew the lace's scalloped edge in place, taking small tucks as you stitch. Stitch together the ends of a 13-inch piece of lace. Sew a gathering row along the straight edge, and gather the lace to fit the small circle. Stitch the lace flat against the pillow top.

4. Button: Stitch ¼ inch from the edges of the small satin circle. Turn under the edge on the stitchline, and slipstitch the "button" to the pillow top, overlapping the inner edges of the small lace circle *(see Stitch Guide, page 146)*.

5. Ruffle: Stitch together the ends of the satin strips to make a loop. Fold the loop in half lengthwise, wrong sides together, and press. Pin a 45-inch length of lace to the loop, with the scalloped edge ⅜ inch from the fold; stitch along the lace's straight edge. Sew gathering rows ¼ and ⅝ inch from the loop's raw edges. Gather the ruffle to fit the pillow top, and stitch, right sides together and edges matching.

6. Assembly: Pin the second batting circle to the wrong side of the pillow back. Pin the back to the pillow top, right sides together, ruffle inside toward the center. Stitch together leaving a 5-inch opening. Turn right side out, stuff lightly and slipstitch the opening closed. Take four stitches through pillow center to indent.

NIGHTGOWN CASE DIRECTIONS:

1. Cutting: From satin, cut two 14 x 45-inch rectangles. **From batting,** cut one 14 x 45-inch rectangle.

2. Case: Place the satin pieces, right sides together and edges matching, on top of the batting. Stitch together the layers around three sides and four corners. Trim the batting. Turn case right side out; slipstitch the opening closed *(see Stitch Guide)*.

3. Lace Trim: Topstitch around the case, ⅜ inch from the edges. Pin lace around the top of the case, mitering the corners, with the straight edge just inside the stitchline. Sew the lace to the case. Add a second piece of lace in the same way, with the straight edge ¼ inch beyond the scalloped edge of the first piece.

4. Tie Quilting: Thread the needle with embroidery floss; do not knot the floss. Take a stitch through all three layers, leaving a 1-inch tail. Cut the floss 1 inch above the fabric. Tie the tails in a square knot *(see How to Tie a Square Knot, page 145)*; trim the ends to ½ inch. Repeat across case, spacing ties 1½ inches apart.

5. Finishing: Place the case lace side down. Fold one short end 10 inches toward the center, and stitch over both side edges to make a pocket. Repeat at the opposite end to make a second pocket.

STOCKING CASE DIRECTIONS:

1. Cutting: From satin, cut two 11½ x 24½-inch rectangles. **From batting,** cut one 11½ x 24½-inch rectangle.

2. Assembly: Following Steps 2 to 5 of Nightgown Case, make the Stocking Case with one lace row and one 8-inch pocket.

POCKET CASE DIRECTIONS:

1. Cutting: From satin, cut two 12½ x 35- and three 11½ x 17-inch rectangles. **From batting,** cut one 12½ x 35-inch rectangle.

2. Assembly: Following Steps 2 to 4 of Nightgown Case, make the outer case using the large satin and batting pieces.

3. Pockets: Fold a small rectangle in half, right sides together and short edges matching. Stitch along the raw edges leaving a 2-inch opening. Turn right side out and slipstitch the opening closed. Stitch lace along the top edge of the pocket. Repeat to make two more pockets. Slipstitch the pockets to the inside of the case, spacing them evenly.

AVERAGE:
For those with some experience in quilting.

DIMENSIONS:
Pillow, 13" diameter; nightgown case, 13 x 24"; stocking case, 10½ x 8", folded; pocket case, 11½ x 34", unfolded (not shown in photo on page 120)

MATERIALS:
To make pillow, nightgown case, stocking case and pocket case:
- 3 yards of 45-inch-wide ivory polyester satin
- 10 yards of 1⅜-inch-wide ivory scallop-edged lace
- matching sewing thread
- 1½ yards of 45-inch-wide synthetic batting
- ½ yard of 45-inch-wide muslin
- synthetic stuffing
- dressmaker's pencil
- ivory embroidery floss
- large embroidery needle
- large embroidery hoop
- Basic Quilting Tools, page 137

JACOB'S LADDER TABLE RUNNER

A purely patchwork project for people who love to piece! The colors of fabric used to make Jacob's Ladder Table Runner are a bit unusual, but the pattern is a classic that would make a lovely addition to a real country kitchen or dining room.

DIRECTIONS:
(¼-inch seams allowed)

1. Patterns: On the crisp cardboard or manila folders, draw one 6-inch square, one 3-inch square and one right triangle with two 6-inch sides; be sure the corners are exactly 90°. Cut out the patterns.

2. Cutting: Place the pattern templates on the wrong side of the fabrics, and trace around the edges with a sharp dressmaker's pencil. Cut out each piece ¼ inch beyond the drawn lines for a seam allowance. **From the white fabric,** cut forty 3-inch squares. **From the royal blue fabric,** cut forty 3-inch squares. **From the aqua fabric,** cut twenty triangles with the long edge on the straight of the fabric grain. **From the peach fabric,** cut thirty-six triangles with one short edge on the straight of the fabric grain. **From the bright yellow fabric,** cut nine 6-inch squares. **From the backing fabric,** cut two 30 x 33-inch rectangles and one 30-inch square.

3. Piecing: For greatest accuracy, pin or baste the pieces together before stitching. Press each seam toward the darker fabric before adding another patch. With right sides together and drawn lines matching, stitch a white square to a blue square. Repeat to make a total of 40 white/blue rectangles. Stitch together two white/blue rectangles along a long edge to make a large square, placing the rectangles so the colors alternate. Repeat to make a total of 20 white/blue large squares. Set aside two white/blue large squares for the runner ends. Stitch the short edge of a peach triangle to one side of the remaining white/blue large squares. Stitch a second peach triangle to the adjoining edge of the square as shown in FIG. IV, 4A to make a large triangle with a white/blue square as the center point. Repeat to make a total of 18 large triangles. Using the photo as a guide, stitch together 9 large triangles with the first and last triangles in the row pointing the same direction. Repeat to make a second row of 9 large triangles. Following FIG. IV, 4B, stitch together the yellow squares and the aqua triangles to make the center strip. Stitch a reserved white/blue large square to either end of the yellow/aqua center strip (*see* FIG. IV, 4B). Stitch together the three pieced strips along their long edges, matching the long raw edges of the aqua and peach triangles.

4. Runner Back: Stitch together the three backing pieces along their short ends, placing the 30-inch square in the center.

4. Assembly: Place the runner back, right side up, on a clean, flat surface. Place the runner top, wrong side up and centered, on top of the runner back. Trim the edges of runner back to match the runner top. Stitch together the runner top and back around all the edges, leaving a 10-inch opening along one long edge for turning. Turn the table runner right side out, and slipstitch the opening closed (*see Stitch Guide, page 146*).

QUILTS FROM THE GOOD BOOK

The strong religious influences of the 19th century were apparent in many aspects of daily life, so it is not surprising that stories from the Bible provided inspiration for many quilt makers. The motifs ranged from abstract patterns, such as Jacob's Ladder, Job's Tears, Crown of Thorns and Star of Bethlehem, to pictorial quilts that might include scenes from the life of Christ, Noah's Ark and Jonah and the Whale.

AVERAGE:
For those with some experience in patchwork.

DIMENSIONS:
About 26½ x 94½"

MATERIALS:
- 45-inch-wide cotton poplin: ¾ yard of peach; ¾ yard of aqua; ½ yard each of royal blue, bright yellow and white; 2½ yards of backing fabric
- matching sewing threads
- crisp cardboard or manila folders
- dressmaker's pencil
- Basic Quilting Tools, page 137

FIG. IV, 4A
OUTER BORDER PIECING DIAGRAM

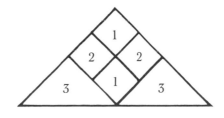

1 = BLUE SQUARE
2 = WHITE SQUARE
3 = PEACH TRIANGLE
4 = AQUA TRIANGLE
5 = YELLOW SQUARE

FIG. IV, 4B
MIDDLE PIECING DIAGRAM

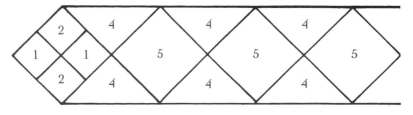

TRAPUNTO AND ACCENT PILLOWS

TRAPUNTO AND ACCENT PILLOWS

The decorative relief stitching technique known as trapunto quilting is a centuries-old art. The name comes from the Italian "trapungere," meaning "to embroider."

Trapunto quilting is done to create a relief design on fabric, not to anchor a piece of batting. A design outline is stitched on the top fabric, then stuffed from behind to make the design stand out. The remaining fabric on the piece is not stuffed. A quilter can create a variety of effects depending on the amount of stuffing used for each motif.

The Trapunto Pillow shown at left uses a printed fabric as the basis for the quilted motif. This is a modern approach to a traditional art. Most antique trapunto pieces were done on solid color fabric. The elaborate designs were created only by stitching and stuffing.

In 17th and 18th century Europe, trapunto was used to decorate petticoats, caps and other garments, as well as for bedcovers. Because it was meant to be purely decorative, trapunto was often done on fine fabrics such as silk.

Making this Trapunto Pillow will acquaint you with the technique. Having mastered the skill, try trapunto work on solid color fabrics using a favorite quilting pattern.

TRAPUNTO QUILTED PILLOW DIRECTIONS:

(½-inch seams allowed)

1. Cutting: From the floral fabric, cut one 11 x 12-inch piece with a flower motif in the center and a 1⅝ x 44-inch bias strip, pieced as needed. **From the contrasting fabric,** cut one 11 x 12-inch pillow back. **From the muslin,** cut a piece 1 inch larger all around than the center flower motif.

2. Trapunto: Baste the muslin piece to the back of the floral fabric piece, placing the muslin so that it covers the center flower motif area. Working from the top, backstitch over the outside edges of the center flower motif petals *(see Stitch Guide, page 146)*. Cut a small slit in the muslin behind each petal section and stuff the section until it is the desired height. Sew the openings closed.

3. Bias Covered Welting: Make a 44-inch-long piece of bias covered welting following the directions on page 144. Pin the welting around the edges of the pillow top, matching the raw edges. Using a zipper foot, stitch the welting to the pillow top.

4. Assembly: With right sides together, raw edges matching and the welting inside toward the center, stitch the pillow back to the pillow top around three sides and four corners, leaving an opening for turning on one side edge. Turn the pillow right side out, stuff it firmly and slipstitch the opening closed *(see Stitch Guide)*.

RECTANGULAR PILLOWS DIRECTIONS:

(½-inch seams allowed)

1. Cutting: From the floral or other print fabric, cut one 9 x 13-inch rectangle for the large pillow or one 9 x 10-inch rectangle for the small pillow. **From the contrasting fabric,** cut one 9 x 13-inch rectangle for the large pillow or one 9 x 10-inch rectangle for the small pillow.

2. Assembly: With right sides together and raw edges even, stitch together the pillow top and pillow back pieces around three sides and four corners, leaving an opening on one short side edge for turning. Turn the pillow right side out, stuff it firmly and slipstitch the opening closed *(see Stitch Guide)*.

AVERAGE:
For those with some experience in quilting.

DIMENSIONS:
Trapunto quilted pillow, 10 x 11"; large rectangular pillow, 8 x 12", small rectangular pillow, 8 x 9" large bolster, 11" long, small bolster 9½" long; heart-shaped pillow, 8 x 9"

MATERIALS:
To make one pillow:
- 45-inch-wide fabric: ⅔ yard of floral print or other print; ⅔ yard of contrasting fabric for pillow back
- matching sewing threads
- scraps of muslin
- 1¼ yards of cording
- synthetic stuffing
- cotton string
- safety pin
- tracing paper
- Basic Quilting Tools, page 137

TRAPUNTO
AND
ACCENT
PILLOWS

BOLSTER PILLOWS DIRECTIONS:
(½-inch seams allowed)

1. Cutting: From floral or other print fabric, cut one 12 x 14-inch rectangle for the large bolster pillow or one 9½ x 10-inch rectangle for the small bolster pillow.

2. Assembly: Fold the large or small rectangle in half lengthwise, right sides together and long raw edges matching. Stitch the long edges of the rectangle to make a tube. Press the seam to one side. Turn a short raw edge ¼ inch to the wrong side of the fabric, press in place, then fold again 1 inch. Stitch the hem close to the fold, leaving a ½-inch opening along the seam. Stitch again ½ inch from the edge to form a casing. Repeat at the opposite short end.

3. Finishing: Tie the end of a piece of string to a safety pin, and insert the pin through the opening on a casing. Maneuver the pin through the casing until it comes out of the other end of the opening. Pull the string until the casing is gathered and the opening is closed. Tie the ends of the string in a square knot *(see How to Tie a Square Knot, page 145)*, and trim the ends to about 1 inch. Repeat at the other end of the pillow but do not pull up the string. Stuff the pillow firmly through the open end, then pull the string as tight as possible and tie it securely. Tuck the string ends and casing edges inside the pillow ends.

HEART-SHAPED PILLOW DIRECTIONS:
(½-inch seams allowed)

1. Pattern: Fold a piece of tracing paper in half. Place the folded edge along the dotted line of the full-size half-heart pattern in Fig. IV, 5. Trace the pattern, then add a second line ½inch beyond the first for a seam allowance. Cut out the pattern on the second line and open the paper for a full pattern.

2. Cutting: From the floral fabric, cut one heart and a 4 x 60-inch ruffle. **From the contrasting fabric,** cut one heart.

3. Ruffle: Turn one long edge and two short ends of the ruffle strip ¼ inch to the wrong side and press, then turn the pressed edges ¼ inch more. Stitch along the long and short folded edges to make a hem. Stitch a gathering row ½ inch from the long raw edge. Stitch a second gathering row ¼ inch from the first row. Fold the ruffle strip in half to find the center, and mark the center point. Pin the ruffle strip's center point to the bottom point of the floral fabric heart, right sides together and edges matching. Pin the short ends of the ruffle strip to the floral heart's top center indentation. Pull up the gathers to fit the ruffle to the heart, distributing the gathers more fully at the bottom point of the heart. Stitch the ruffle to the floral heart.

4. Assembly: Pin the second fabric heart to the floral fabric heart, right sides together, raw edges matching and the ruffle inside toward the center. Stitch together the hearts leaving a 5-inch opening on one side edge for turning. Clip the top indentation almost to the seamline. Make several additional cuts along the curves of the heart. Turn the heart pillow right side out, stuff it firmly and slipstitch the opening closed *(see Stitch Guide, page 146)*.

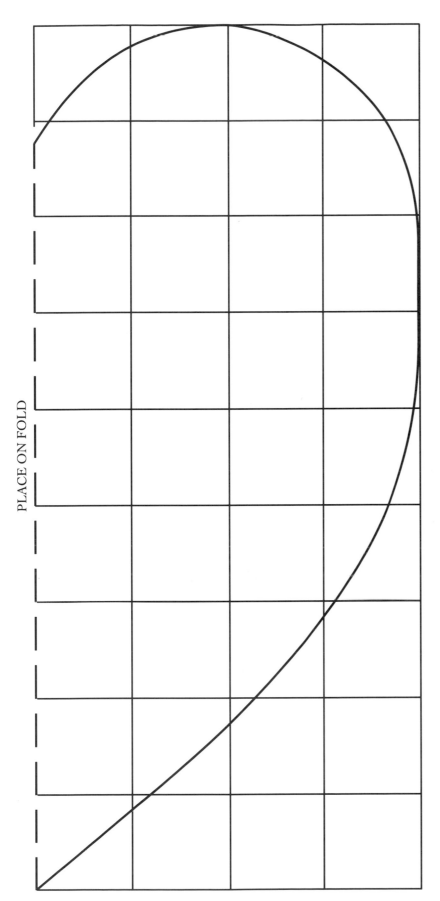

PLACE ON FOLD

FIG. IV, 5   HALF HEART PATTERN   FULL SIZE

Because of their small size, pillows are ideal projects for experimenting with techniques. Making a pillow is less intimidating than stitching an entire quilt, particularly when learning a tricky technique like trapunto.

In the 17th and 18th centuries, trapunto work was as elaborate as very fine embroidery. These quilts were often white-on-white. A piece of fine white fabric was backed with loosely woven fabric. Working from the top and using white thread, the layers were decoratively quilted. The threads of the backing fabric were gently opened, but not cut, and bits of stuffing were inserted behind the stitched designs. The stuffing often was done with a tapestry needle. When the design was completely stuffed, the backing threads were carefully moved back into place.

SUNBURST PILLOW

AVERAGE:
For those with some experience in sewing.

DIMENSIONS:
About 18″ square

MATERIALS:
- 45-inch-wide cotton: 1 yard each of complementary shades of pale yellow, gold, yellow, beige and white; ⅓ yard total pale yellow and gold for borders
- matching sewing threads
- ½ yard of muslin
- crisp cardboard or manila folders
- 18-inch-square pillow form
- dressmaker's pencil
- compass
- Basic Quilting Tools, page 137

A new technique that produces dramatic results. The folding and layering of patches used to make the Sunburst Pillows creates bright, beautiful three-dimensional patchwork. Although the pillows look complicated, they actually are fairly simple to make.

The pillows in the photo at right were made with complementary shades of yellow and gold, accented with white, to capture the brilliance of the summer sun. Different color combinations will yield an entirely different result. Made with shades of pink and rose, the pattern takes on a floral quality. Combining black, rust, royal blue, slate and peach patches will give the pillows a Southwestern flavor.

The same patchwork technique can be used to create a quilt top. Eight quilt blocks are needed to make a twin-size quilt top; twelve blocks will make a full-size quilt. Just add drops to both side edges and to the bottom edge of the quilt top. To carry the radiant effect of the blocks onto the drops, stitch together strips of the same complementary-colored fabrics used to make the quilt blocks. Stitch a strip of the lightest color next to the quilt top, and add deeper shades as you stitch.

DIRECTIONS:

1. Pattern: Using the compass, draw a 3-inch-diameter circle on the crisp cardboard or manila folders, and cut out the circle pattern.

2. Cutting: To save time, pin the fabric in layers (*no more than eight layers at a time*) and, using the pattern, trace the circle on the top layer. Place a pin in the center of the drawn circle and down through the remaining layers. Cut out the circle through all the layers. **From the gold fabric,** cut 18 circles. **From the yellow fabric,** cut 72 circles. **From the pale yellow fabric,** cut 60 circles and two 13 x 19-inch pillow back pieces. **From the beige fabric,** cut 68 circles. **From the white fabric,** cut 132 circles. **From the muslin,** cut one 13-inch square. **From the border fabric,** cut four 4 x 13-inch strips and four 4-inch squares from gold or pale yellow in combination desired.

3. Marking: Using the dressmaker's pencil, lightly draw diagonal lines connecting the corners of the muslin square. The diagonal lines will be used as placement guides. Mark the center point. Place the circle pattern in the center of the square and trace around it (*see* FIG. IV, 6A, *page 130*). Place the dressmaker's pencil in the compass. With the point of the compass at the center point of the square, draw 9 concentric circles beyond the center circle, spacing the circles a generous ½ inch apart.

4. Cone Patches: Fold one of the gold fabric circles in half, raw edges matching. Using FIG. IV, 6B (*page 130*) as a guide, fold the half circle in thirds, overlapping the edges to make a cone shape. Finger-press the folded edges to make a point on the cone. Fold and pin the circles following the order in Step 5, below.

5. Patchwork: Round 1: Pin six gold cones along the center circle on the muslin square. The rounded edges of the cones should match the drawn circle lines, and the cone points should meet in the middle of the square (*see* FIG. IV, 6C, *page 131*). Stitch the cones to the muslin square ¼ inch from the raw edges of the cones. **Round 2:** Working counterclockwise, in the same way pin and stitch 12 gold cones to the muslin square along the second drawn circle, ½ inch beyond the first

(Continued on page 130)

SUNBURST PILLOW

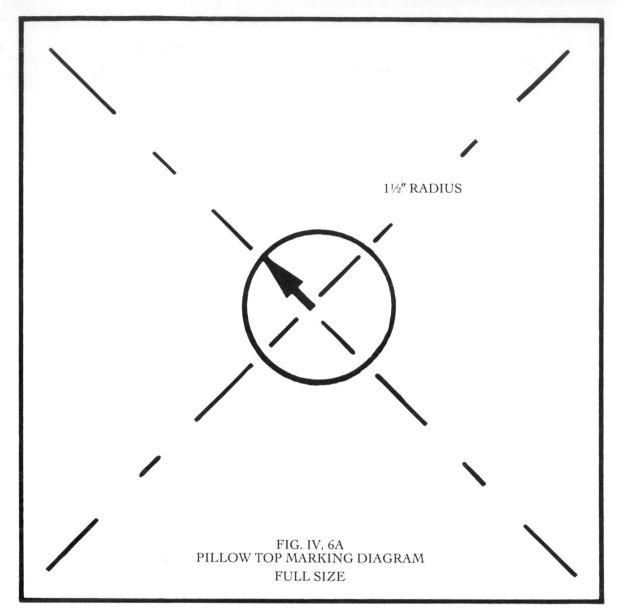

1½″ RADIUS

FIG. IV, 6A
PILLOW TOP MARKING DIAGRAM
FULL SIZE

**SUNBURST
PILLOW**

round. Slightly overlap the edges of the gold points as needed to space the cones evenly around the circle. Continue to add circles of cones as follows, using the photo on page 129 and FIG. IV, 6C as guides. **Rounds 3 and 4:** Yellow. **Rounds 5 and 6:** Pale yellow. **Rounds 7 and 8:** Beige with a yellow inserted on each diagonal line. **Rounds 9 and 10:** White with a yellow inserted on each diagonal line. Fill in the corners with curved rows of white, inserting yellow cones on the diagonal lines (*see photo*). Trim the overhanging curved cone edges flush with the edges of the muslin square.

6. Borders: Stitch a border strip to opposite sides of the patchwork block. Stitch a border square to both short ends of the remaining two border strips, and stitch

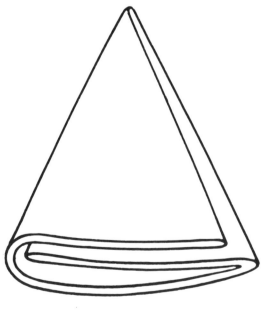

FIG. IV, 6B
CIRCLE FOLDING DIAGRAM

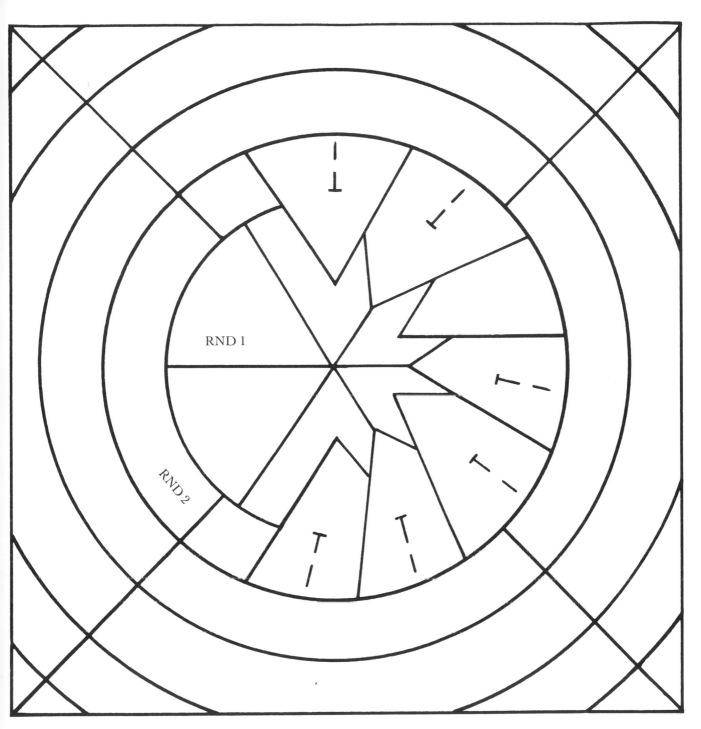

RND 1

RND 2

the combined strips to the long edges of the combined patchwork block and borders to complete the pillow top.

7. Pillow Back: Stitch a ½-inch hem along one long edge of each pillow back piece. Place both pillow back pieces on a flat surface, right sides up and raw edges even, and lap one hemmed edge over the other until the pillow back is the same size as the pillow top. Pin the lapped edges in place, then stitch together the pillow back pieces along the edges of the overlap. Leave the hemmed long edges open.

8 . Assembly: With right sides together and raw edges even, stitch the pillow top to the pillow back around four sides and corners. Clip the corners and turn the pillow right side out through the hemmed opening at the center back. Insert the pillow form.

FIG. IV, 6C
PILLOW TOP
ASSEMBLY DIAGRAM

VARIABLE STAR TABLE RUNNER

EASY:
Achievable by anyone.

DIMENSIONS:
About 19 x 50"

MATERIALS:
- 44-inch-wide cotton:
  ¼ yard each of beige,
  medium brown and
  dark brown calico;
  1 yard of brown print;
  1½ yards of solid
  brown for runner back
- matching sewing
  threads
- matching quilting
  threads
- 20 x 50-inch piece of
  lightweight batting
- crisp cardboard
  or manila folders
- dressmaker's pencil
- large embroidery
  hoop or quilting hoop
- Basic Quilting Tools,
  page 137

The Variable Star is one of the simplest patchwork motifs to piece, made even easier because there are only two colors of fabric used to make the star instead of three. This table runner with its eight-point star motif is an excellent choice for the beginning patchworker.

Pieced from triangles and squares, the Variable Star is the basis for many other patchwork designs. To add more interest to the pattern, cut four triangle patches from a different fabric and use them as the horizontal triangles in the motif. Or cut the four triangles from the same fabric used to make the center square. By careful color choice and patch placement, one simple motif can evolve into many different designs.

Having mastered the basic piecing of the Variable Star, experiment with color. Reverse the light and dark patches in the project. Try red, white and blue fabrics to make a table runner for the Forth of July, or use red, white and green to create the perfect table setting for Christmas Dinner. For an Amish look, piece the runner from patches of solid black, royal blue and burgundy fabrics.

DIRECTIONS:
(¼-inch seams allowed)

1. Patterns: On the crisp cardboard or manila folders, draw a 3¼-inch square and a right triangle with one 4½-inch side and two 3¼-inch sides; be sure the corners are exactly 90°. Cut out the patterns.

2. Cutting: Using the dressmaker's pencil, trace the patterns on the wrong side of the fabrics. Cut out the fabric patches ¼ inch beyond the drawn lines to allow for seams. **From the beige calico,** cut 12 squares and 24 triangles. **From the medium brown calico,** cut 36 triangles. **From the dark brown calico,** cut 12 triangles. **From the brown print,** cut two 4 x 12½-inch border strips, two 3½ x 45-inch border strips and two 3½ x 19-inch border strips. **From the solid brown fabric,** cut two 21 x 52-inch runner back pieces.

3. Piecing: Stitch together two dark brown triangles along a 3¼-inch edge to make a pieced triangle. Repeat with a second pair of triangles. Stitch together the pieced triangles along their long edges to make a 4½-inch square (*see* Fig. IV, 7A, *page 134*). Repeat to make two more pieced squares. Following Fig. IV, 7B (*page 134*), stitch together two medium brown triangles along their 3¼-inch edges. Stitch a third triangle to a beige square along its short edge. Stitch together the assemblies along their long edges to make a pentagon. Repeat to make 11 more pentagons.

4. Blocks: Stitch four pentagons to a pieced square (*see* Fig. IV, 7C, *page 135*). Repeat with the remaining pentagons and pieced squares to make two more assemblies. Stitch together the beige triangles in pairs along a short edge. Following Fig. IV, 7D (*page 135*), stitch the pieced beige triangles between the raw edges of the medium brown triangles in each assembly, pivoting each triangle at the point and matching the seams to make three 12-inch pieced squares.

5. Borders: Stitch a 4 x 12½-inch brown border between each of the pieced squares to make a 12 x 42-inch rectangle. Stitch a 3½ x 45-inch border to each long raw edge of the pieced rectangle. Trim the short border ends flush with the edges of the quilt blocks. Stitch a 3½ x 19-inch border to either short end of the rectangle, and trim the ends flush with the side borders.

(Continued on page 134)

VARIABLE STAR TABLE RUNNER

VARIABLE
STAR
TABLE
RUNNER

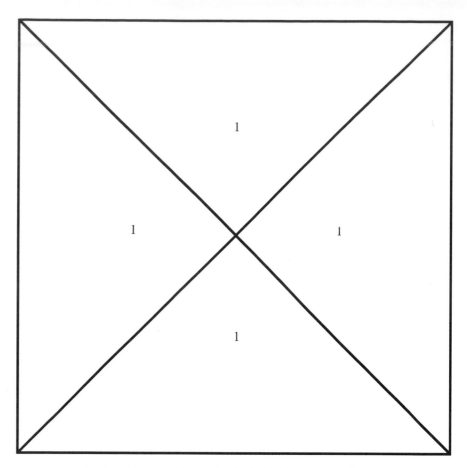

FIG. IV, 7A   PIECING DIAGRAM 1   FULL SIZE

6. Quilting: Spread one runner back piece, wrong side up, on a clean, flat surface. Place the batting, centered, on top of the runner back. Place the pieced runner top, right side up, on top of the batting. Pin-baste through all three layers. Place the runner in a large embroidery hoop or quilting hoop. Starting at the center and using a small running stitch, quilt over the block seams, the dark brown center square seams and around outline of the pieced stars within the blocks. Remove the basting pins.

7. Finishing: Place the second runner back piece, right side up, on a flat surface. Place the quilted runner top, right side down, on top of the runner back, and pin the layers together around the edges. Using a ½-inch seam, stitch together the runner top and back around three sides and four corners, leaving an opening at one end for turning. Remove the pins, turn the runner right side out and press it. Slipstitch the opening closed (*see Stitch Guide, page 146*).

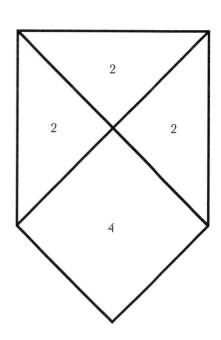

FIG. IV, 7B
PIECING DIAGRAM 2

A TREASURY OF QUILTS

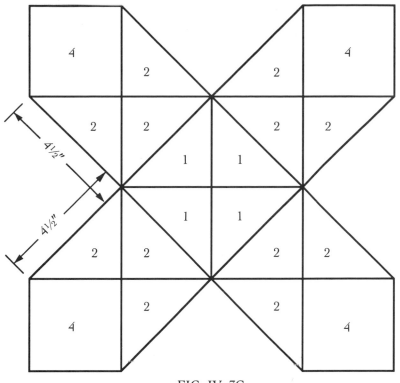

FIG. IV, 7C
PIECING DIAGRAM 3

1 = DARK BROWN TRIANGLE
2 = MED. BROWN TRIANGLE
3 = BEIGE TRIANGLE
4 = BEIGE SQUARE

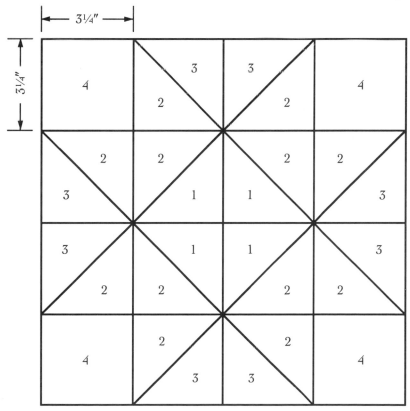

FIG. IV, 7D
PIECING DIAGRAM 4

QUILTING BASICS

BEFORE BEGINNING A QUILTING, PATCHWORK OR APPLIQUÉ PROJECT, IT IS IMPORTANT TO BECOME FAMILIAR WITH THE "TOOLS OF THE TRADE." THIS CHAPTER INTRODUCES THE BEGINNER TO THE SEWING TECHNIQUES AND CRAFTING SUPPLIES THAT QUILTERS USE MOST OFTEN, AND CAN SERVE AS A REFRESHER FOR THE MORE ADVANCED QUILTER.

THERE ARE LISTS OF ITEMS TO HAVE ON HAND WHEN QUILTING, STEP-BY-STEP INSTRUCTIONS TO MAKING PERFECT APPLIQUÉS, AND A VARIETY OF INFORMATION ON BASIC QUILTING SKILLS. ONCE A QUILT IS COMPLETED, PROPER CARE IS NEEDED TO KEEP IT LOOKING BEAUTIFUL FOR YEARS TO COME. FOLLOW THE INSTRUCTIONS ON PAGE 141 TO ENSURE A LONG LIFE FOR ALL YOUR CREATIONS.

KEEP THIS INFORMATION CLOSE AT HAND WHEN QUILTING, DOING PATCHWORK OR APPLIQUÉ. THIS CHAPTER WILL BE A VALUABLE REFERENCE FOR ALL YOUR QUILTING PROJECTS.

CHAPTER

5

BASIC QUILTING TOOLS

A list of "necessaries" — these are items that quilters and patchworkers shouldn't be without. Keep these supplies on hand when quilting, doing patchwork or appliqué projects.

DRESSMAKER'S CARBON AND TRACING WHEEL

Use these tools to transfer patterns directly to fabric when making appliqués, or when cutting only one or two of a particular pattern piece. Trace or enlarge the pattern from the book. Place the dressmaker's carbon, colored side down, on the wrong side of fabric, place the full-size pattern on top of the carbon, and go over the pattern lines with the tracing wheel.

DRESSMAKER'S PENCIL

A pencil specially made for marking fabric, select a pencil whose marks are easily removed. A dressmaker's pencil is useful for tracing patches and appliqué patterns, or marking quilting lines on a project. Use a white pencil to mark dark fabrics; a darker pencil to mark lighter fabrics. Keep the pencil *sharp* to insure accuracy when transferring patterns.

EMBROIDERY FLOSS

A soft, loosely-stranded thread used for decorative needlework on crazy quilts, and to make ties for some tie-quilted projects. Most embroidery floss comes in six-strand skeins, which may be separated or not as per the individual project instructions. For tie-quilting, use all six strands of the floss. Check to be sure the floss is colorfast before beginning a project.

EMBROIDERY SCISSORS

Very sharp, small scissors made expressly for doing delicate, decorative needlework. Use embroidery scissors when cutting lengths of embroidery floss and thread, and to trim the tails on tie-quilted projects. Embroidery scissors also are very useful when doing appliqué work. Use them to trim the appliqué seams, and for clipping corners and patch curves.

IRON

Keep an iron and ironing board handy whenever sewing. Most patchwork projects require patch seams to be pressed as the piecework is done. When possible, press both seams toward the darker fabric so the seams are less visible. Always set the iron carefully to the proper heat for the fabric being pressed.

MASKING TAPE

Masking tape is used to secure the corners of the quilt top or quilt back to hold it in place while arranging and basting the quilt layers together.

MEASURING TOOLS

Precise measuring is essential to fine patchwork; invest in good quality tools to help you measure accurately and neatly. A **ruler** and a **yardstick** are needed to measure and mark patches and quilt borders. A **T-square** or **drafting triangle** is necessary to make the corners of square and triangular patches exactly 90°. A **compass** is needed to make circular patches and curved appliqués. Substitute a dressmaker's pencil for the regular lead pencil in the compass.

NEEDLES

Sewing needles of all sizes are used for simple stitching. A short, sharp size 8 or 9 needle is recommended for quilting, although some quilters prefer a longer needle; do not change needles in the middle of a quilt or the stitching will look uneven. For decorative needlework, have several sizes of **embroidery** needles on hand. For basting together quilt layers, use a **darner** or **milliner's** needle. A **darner** or **curved** needle works best for tie-quilting.

PINS

As with all sewing projects, **straight** pins are needed in quantity. To make keeping track of straight pins easier, use pins with colored heads. **Safety** or **quilter's** pins are used to hold the quilt layers together when stitching around the sides of the quilt or when quilting. This is called pin-basting, and cannot be done with straight pins.

QUILTING HOOP OR FRAME

To help keep quilting stitches even, place the project in a hoop or frame to keep the work taut while stitching. For smaller projects, use a hand-held quilting hoop or a large embroidery hoop. For full-size quilts, invest in a free-standing quilting frame. Quilting frames usually are available at fabric or craft stores. Always begin stitching at the center of the piece, and work out toward the edges.

QUILTING THREAD

Recommended for both hand- and machine-quilting, quilting thread is smoother, stronger and less likely to kink or knot than standard sewing thread. Quilting thread usually can be found in fabric or craft stores. If it is unavailable, substitute heavy-duty mercerized thread, or No. 50, 60 or 70 sewing thread. Running the heavy-duty or sewing thread over a cake of beeswax before stitching will help to smooth it. Wipe off the excess wax before you begin to sew.

When purchasing quilting thread, the choice of color may be limited. If there is no thread to match the fabric, select a color that either complements or contrasts with the fabric. When in doubt, choose white thread to add a touch of old-time authenticity. Most antique quilts were quilted with white thread, regardless of the color of the fabrics.

BEST BETS FOR BATTING

Synthetic batting is recommended for all the quilting projects in this book because it is both washable and long-lasting. Synthetic batting is available on bolts and pre-cut in packages, usually sized for beds from crib to king-size.

Although cotton or wool batting was used in days gone by, they can be difficult to work with and may make the quilt hard to clean. Natural fiber battings tend to separate, shift and clump inside the quilt. To prevent this, the quilting lines should be close together, and unstitched areas should be limited.

SCISSORS

For quilting, patchwork and appliqué projects, have at least two pairs of scissors available: one for cutting the fabric and one for cutting out the cardboard and paper patterns. *Never* use fabric shears to cut paper; this dulls the edges very quickly. Dull scissors do not cut through fabric well, and patch and appliqué measurements may be off because of this.

To sharpen slightly dull scissors quickly, cut through a piece of fine-grade sandpaper five or six times. The grains of sand will hone the edge of the scissors. If the scissors are very dull, use a knife sharpener, or bring them to a fabric center or hardware store for a professional sharpening.

To remove rust from scissors, pour household ammonia on the rusty spots and let it sit for several minutes. Wipe the scissors clean with a cotton rag. Repeat the procedure as needed until all the rust spots have disappeared. Do not try to scrape off rust with steel wool or an abrasive cleaner; this can cause sparking, and may damage the scissors.

TEMPLATE MATERIALS

Most of the projects in this book call for **crisp cardboard** or **manila folders** as a template material. These are inexpensive, easily available materials, and work well for most patterns. If a project calls for a great number of same-size patches or appliqué pieces, **flexible, transparent plastic** is a better choice. To cut templates, use a **craft knife** or an **X-acto®** blade; they are more accurate than scissors for fine cutting. **Tracing paper** is needed for tracing or enlarging patterns, and **carbon paper** is useful for transferring the tracing paper patterns onto the template material. Or cut out the tracing paper patterns, use a **glue stick** to attach them to the template material, and cut out the template patterns.

Using a dressmaker's pencil, trace around the outside of the templates onto the back of the fabric to make the patches or appliqués. Before cutting out the fabric pieces, check the project directions carefully to see whether the drawn line is the *cutting* line or the *stitching* line. If it is the stitching line, add the seam allowance by cutting out the patches ¼ inch beyond the drawn lines.

To make templates for quilting designs, cut the patterns from the cardboard or plastic material as for a stencil. To transfer the quilting lines to the fabric, trace *inside* the template cutouts.

THE FABRIC SELECTION

The following are some general guidelines to selecting fabrics for quilting projects.

Select fabric with prints in proportion to the size of the patchwork and appliqué pieces. Make templates for patches before buying the fabric, and bring the templates along when shopping. Use the size of the templates to determine the overall effect of a particular print within a complete project.

Check out the bins of fabric seconds and end-of-bolt specials at the fabric store. These often contain great bargains, and many fabric defects can be cut around for patchwork.

Buy extra fabric in case of mistakes. Leftover pieces of fabric can easily be incorporated into other patchwork projects. Or use fabric leftovers to make a pillow to match the quilt.

Check the fabric content, and select *only* washable fabrics, especially for baby quilts.

Wash all cotton and cotton blend fabrics to pre-shrink and test them for colorfastness before cutting the fabrics.

Always press fabrics before marking them for cutting.

QUILT SIZES

In days gone by, a bed was custom-made to fit the owner; there were no standard sizes of beds. Accordingly, there were no standard sizes of bedcovers; antique quilts come in all shapes and sizes. Today, there are standards for both beds and bedcovers. Quilts for modern beds should be made with a minimum 10-inch drop on either side and at the foot. The following will help to translate bed footage into quilt sizing.

STANDARD BED MEASUREMENTS

To determine the sizing of a quilt, begin by measuring the bed it will cover, or a reasonable estimation thereof.
Standard mattress sizes:

> 38 x 72 inches — twin
> 54 x 75 inches — double
> 60 x 80 inches — queen
> 72 x 84 inches — king

To make a quilt with a 10-inch drop on either side and at the foot, add 20 inches to the width measurement of the quilt top, and 10 inches to the length.
For a quilt with a 10-inch drop:

> 58 x 82 inches — twin
> 74 x 85 inches — double
> 80 x 90 inches — queen
> 92 x 94 inches — king

If you want the quilt to touch the floor, add at least a 20-inch drop on either side and at the foot. Add 40 inches to the width measurement of the quilt top, and 20 inches to the length.
For a quilt with a 20-inch drop:

> 78 x 92 inches — twin
> 94 x 95 inches — double
> 100 x 100 inches — queen
> 112 x 104 inches — king

Always measure the height of the bed, just to be sure the drop on the quilt is correct. Heights will vary depending on the type of mattress, whether the bed is on casters, on a platform or on a carpeted or tiled floor. Antique beds tend to be higher off the ground than modern beds.

CRIB MEASUREMENTS

A standard-sized crib mattress measures 27 x 52 inches. Crib quilts do not require drops, but allow enough fabric around the edges of the quilt top so the quilt can be tucked under the mattress.

WALL HANGINGS AND MINI-QUILTS

The sizing of a wall hanging or mini-quilt is entirely at the discretion of the quilter. The size will be determined by the design, and can be made larger or smaller by adding or removing borders around the quilt top.

CARING FOR QUILTS

Whether you own an antique quilt or have created your own heirloom-quality quilt, follow these tips to care for quilts so they may be enjoyed for years to come.

AIRING QUILTS

The safest method for airing a quilt that is 50 or more years old is to place it outdoors in the shade on a clear, dry, breezy day. Never hang a quilt on a clothesline; this weakens the stitches. To air a quilt indoors, set several same-size chairs side-by-side, drape the quilt over the chairs, and let it stand for half a day.

CLEANING QUILTS

To vacuum: Cover the edges of a 24-inch square of fiberglass screening with masking tape. Lay the quilt flat on a bed or other clean surface, and place the fiberglass screen on top of the quilt. Using a low-power, hand-held vacuum with a clean brush attachment, slowly and gently vacuum over the screened part of the quilt. When the first section is clean, carefully move the screen to another part of the quilt, and repeat the vacuuming. When the top of the quilt is done, turn back half the quilt and vacuum the bed or surface under it. Repeat with the other half of the quilt. Turn over the quilt, and repeat the screen vacuuming on the back. This method should not be used more than once a year. Never vacuum a quilt with beading on it.

To dry or wet clean: Dry or wet cleaning of a quilt should be done only by an expert who specializes in quilt cleaning. There is no guarantee that either method will work, or that the cleaning process will not damage the quilt.

QUILT STORAGE

Proper storage is essential to the long life of any quilt, whether it's an antique heirloom, or crafted in recent years.

Wrap each quilt in acid-free tissue paper, washed muslin, washed cotton or cotton/polyester-blend sheets. If the quilt has a metal part attached to it, remove the metal, if possible, before wrapping the quilt for storage. Place the wrapped quilt in an acid-free box, or place it in a bureau drawer lined with acid-free tissue paper, washed muslin or clean cotton sheets. If storing the quilt in a bureau, coat the drawer with polyurethane varnish before lining it with the acid-free tissue, muslin or cotton. The polyurethane must be *completely* dry before you line the drawer.

Do not wrap quilts in plastic wrap or bags or Styrofoam®, or in any product made from wood, such as cardboard or regular (not acid-free) tissue paper. This can result in discoloration of the fabric and deterioration of the quilt.

To prevent soil build-up, discoloration and wear, fold the quilt as follows: Fold the quilt into thirds, placing a roll of acid-free tissue paper along and under each fold. Fold the quilt into thirds again, folding toward the center of the quilt, and placing a roll of crumpled acid-free tissue paper along and under each of these two fold lines. Clean cotton sheets or washed muslin may be substituted for the acid-free tissue paper.

Store the boxed quilt in a cool area that is clean, dry, dark and well-ventilated. Relative humidity should be about 50%. Do not store quilts in an attic or basement — the quilts will mildew.

FOOLPROOF APPLIQUÉ

Appliqué is a delicate art, and can be tricky, especially when the appliqués have curved edges. The following is a step-by-step demonstration to take the guesswork out of making appliqués.

DIRECTIONS:

1. Draw or trace the appliqué pattern on crisp cardboard or a manila folder, or on plastic template material, and cut out the pattern. Using a dressmaker's pencil, trace the pattern on the wrong side of the fabric. Do not cut out the fabric shape.

2. To prevent the fabric from raveling, stitch over the traced lines either by hand or machine. Draw a second line ¼ inch beyond the stitched lines for seam allowance; if you wish, make the cutting line a broken line. Cut out the fabric shape on the second drawn line.

3. To make the appliqués lie flat on the quilt top, cut small notches within the seam allowance along the appliqué's curves. Using the tips of the scissors, make small, straight cuts along the straight edges of the appliqués.

4. Using the stitchline as a guide, turn the clipped appliqué edges to the wrong side of the fabric, and press the fold. Using contrasting thread, and a long, loose stitch, baste the appliqué edges in place.

6. Continue to slipstitch the appliqué to the background fabric, stitching around all the edges of the appliqué and spacing the stitches about ⅛-inch apart. Remove the basting threads.

5. Place the appliqué in position on the background fabric. Pin or baste the appliqué to the background fabric in several places. Begin slipstitching the appliqué to the background fabric (*see Stitch Guide, page 146*).

HOW TO MAKE BIAS COVERED WELTING

Welting is used to give a finished edge to pillows, or to reinforce the edges of a quilt top. Using fabric cut on the bias gives added strength to the finished welting. One-half yard of fabric will yield 12 yards of 1⅝-inch-wide bias strips for ¼-inch welting cord, and about 9 yards of 2½-inch-wide bias strips for jumbo (⅜-inch) welting cord.

DIRECTIONS:

1. To Straighten Fabric Edges: Place a newspaper on top of the fabric, matching one straight paper edge to the selvage, or a fabric edge cut parallel to the selvage. Trim the perpendicular edge of the fabric even with the right edge of the paper.

2. Marking and Cutting: Starting at the upper right corner of the fabric, mark a point on the length of the fabric, and a second mark the same distance along the width. Using a dressmaker's pencil and a yardstick, draw a diagonal line connecting the two marks (*see* Fig. V, 1A). Repeat along the entire length and width of the fabric. Cut along the marked lines.

3. Joining: Place two bias strips at right angles to each other, right sides together and the points of the short ends extending (*see* Fig. V, 1B). Stitch together the short ends on the diagonal. Repeat until the bias strip is the desired length. Press the seams open, and cut off the points as shown.

4. Covering the Cord: Fold the bias strip in half lengthwise, wrong sides together and raw edges matching, placing the cord along the inside of the fold. With the corded edge to the left of the zipper foot, stitch down the length of the bias strip as close to the cord as possible, without catching the cord in the stitching.

5. Assembly: Pin the welting to the right side of the fabric piece, raw edges matching. Stitch together the welting and the project fabric, stitching close to the welting cord. Clip the welting up to the stitch line to ease it around the corners. With right sides together and the corded edge toward the center, stitch the welted piece to the back piece using the previous stitching as a stitchline.

6. Overlaps: Where the ends of the welting overlap, trim the cord ends *only* from inside the bias strip.

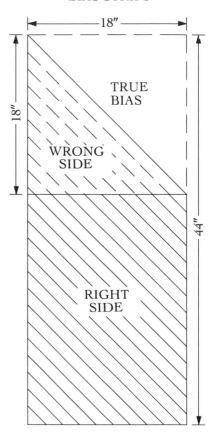

FIG. VI, 1A
CUTTING
BIAS STRIPS

½ YARD OF FABRIC YIELDS 12 YARDS OF 1⅝-INCH-WIDE BIAS STRIPS FOR ¼″ WELTING CORD

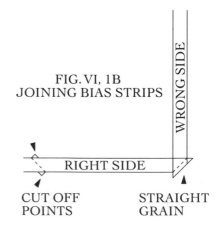

FIG. VI, 1B
JOINING BIAS STRIPS

HOW TO MAKE
A CASING

A casing can be added to any mini-quilt (and to many full-size quilts) to make it into a beautiful and unique wall hanging.

DIRECTIONS:

1. Using the same fabric as the quilt back, cut a strip of fabric 2½ inches wide and about 2 inches shorter than the length of the top edge of the finished quilt.

2. Turn under the short edges of the casing strip ¼ inch, and press the folds. Stitch the folds in place to hem the casing ends.

3. Fold the casing strip in half lengthwise, right sides together and raw edges matching. Stitch together the long edges of the casing, stitching ¼ inch from the raw edges. Turn the casing right side out and press it so the seam becomes the bottom edge. Pin the casing to the quilt back, centered, with the top edge of the casing ½ inch from the top edge of the quilt. Slipstitch the top and bottom edges of the casing to the quilt back (*see Stitch Guide, page 146*). Slide a sturdy dowel that is at least ⅝ inch in diameter and the same length as the top edge of the quilt through the casing for hanging.

HOW TO ENLARGE PATTERNS

On a sheet of tracing paper or brown paper, draw a grid with squares measuring the size specified in the pattern (i.e., 1 square = 1 inch). Following the grid drawn on the pattern, copy the pattern square by square onto the larger grid.

You might find it easier to use a drafting tool called a *pantograph* to enlarge designs. The pantograph resembles an accordian-pleated coat rack with two pencils attached. To use the pantograph, trace the actual drawing with one pencil while the second pencil redraws the image on a larger scale. This tool is available at art supply stores.

The simplest way to enlarge patterns is to use a photocopying machine with an enlargement setting. Follow the grid enlargement measurement given in the original drawing, and be sure to check the enlarged photocopy for accuracy.

HOW TO TIE
A SQUARE KNOT

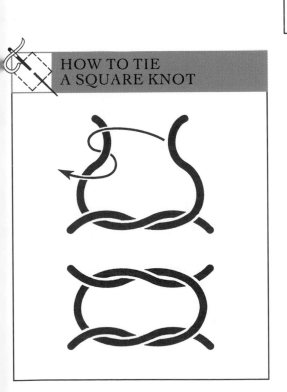

STITCH GUIDE

BACKSTITCH

CHAIN STITCH

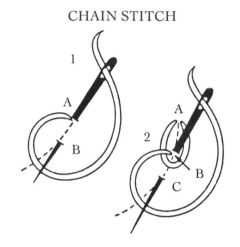

BUTTONHOLE STITCH

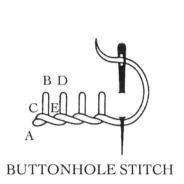

CROSS STITCH

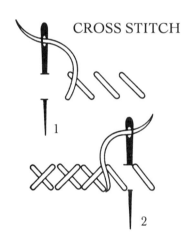

FLY STITCH

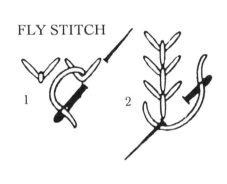

HERRINGBONE STITCH

FEATHER STITCH

FRENCH KNOT

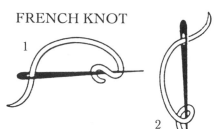

OVERCAST STITCH

SATIN STITCH

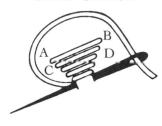

SLIPSTITCH

STEM STITCH

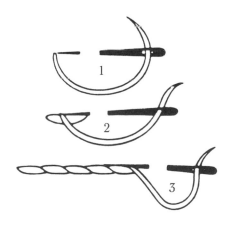

BLIND STITCH

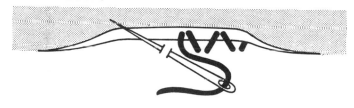

QUILTING STITCH (RUNNING STITCH)

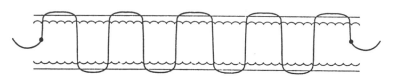

INDEX

Italicized Page Numbers
Refer to Photographs

T ✳ ✳ ✳ ✳ ✳

V ✳ ✳ ✳ ✳ ✳

W ✳ ✳ ✳ ✳ ✳

CONTRIBUTING CRAFT EDITORS

Joanne Beretta: Page 92

Ann Boyce: Page 83

Abby Lee Bringman: Page 101

Roxie Curb: Page 129

Jackie Curry: Pages 30-31

Barbara Esposito: Pages 75, 105

Ann Leggiero Kelly: Page 124

Marlene Koenig: Page 133

Michelle & Danielle Koenig: Page 41

Jean Ray Laury: Page 35

Manhattan Quilter's Guild: Pages 23, 45, 71

Phoebe McNuff: Page 14

Marti Michell: Page 57, 63, 67

Kim Mulky of 31 West Studios: Pages 108-109

Courtesy of Winterthur Museum: Page 7

Nina Pellegrini: Page 115

Kathleen Sharp: Page 47

Mimi Shimmin: Page 19

Constance Spates: Pages 25, 120, 122

Charlyne Stewart: Page 89

Diane E. Troy: Page 54

Special thanks to Marti Michell for her help and cooperation.

PHOTOGRAPHY CREDITS

David Bishop: Page 47

Richard Blinkoff: Page 105

Ralph Bogertman: Pages 14, 92

Gary Denys: Pages 51, 57, 67

Mort Mace: Page 35

Bill McGinn: Pages 25, 54, 63, 75, 79,
92, 101, 108-109, 120, 122, 129, 133 & cover photo

Rudy Muller: Pages 2-3, 7, 11, 19

Leonard Nones: Pages 23, 30-31, 45, 71

Frances Pellegrini: Pages 101, 120

Carin Riley: Pages 142-143

Bob Stoller: Page 124

Michel Tcherevkoff: Page 115

Rene Velez: Pages 54, 83, 92, 101, 108-109, 120, 122, 133

Ken Whitmore: Pages 75, 89